WRITING A PROGRESSIVE PAST

LAUER SERIES IN RHETORIC AND COMPOSITION
Series Editors: Catherine Hobbs, Patricia Sullivan, Thomas Rickert, and Jennifer Bay

The Lauer Series in Rhetoric and Composition honors the contributions Janice Lauer has made to the emergence of Rhetoric and Composition as a disciplinary study. It publishes scholarship that carries on Professor Lauer's varied work in the history of written rhetoric, disciplinarity in composition studies, contemporary pedagogical theory, and written literacy theory and research.

OTHER BOOKS IN THE SERIES

Greek Rhetoric Before Aristotle, 2e, Revised and Expanded Edition by Richard Leo Enos
Rhetoric's Earthly Realm: Heidegger, Sophistry, and the Gorgian Kairos by Bernard Alan Miller (2011)
Techne, from Neoclassicism to Postmodernism: Understanding Writing as a Useful, Teachable Art by Kelly Pender (2011)
Walking and Talking Feminist Rhetorics: Landmark Essays and Controversies, edited by Lindal Buchanan and Kathleen J. Ryan (2010)
Transforming English Studies: New Voices in an Emerging Genre, edited by Lori Ostergaard, Jeff Ludwig, and Jim Nugent (2009)
Ancient Non-Greek Rhetorics, edited by Carol S. Lipson and Roberta A. Binkley (2009)
Roman Rhetoric: Revolution and the Greek Influence, Revised and Expanded Edition, by Richard Leo Enos (2008)
Stories of Mentoring: Theory and Praxis, edited by Michelle F. Eble and Lynée Lewis Gaillet (2008)
Writers Without Borders: Writing and Teaching in Troubled Times by Lynn Z. Bloom (2008)
1977: A Cultural Moment in Composition, by Brent Henze, Jack Selzer, and Wendy Sharer (2008)
The Promise and Perils of Writing Program Administration, edited by Theresa Enos and Shane Borrowman (2008)
Untenured Faculty as Writing Program Administrators: Institutional Practices and Politics, edited by Debra Frank Dew and Alice Horning (2007)
Networked Process: Dissolving Boundaries of Process and Post-Process by Helen Foster (2007)
Composing a Community: A History of Writing Across the Curriculum, edited by Susan H. McLeod and Margot Iris Soven (2006)
Historical Studies of Writing Program Administration: Individuals, Communities, and the Formation of a Discipline, edited by Barbara L'Eplattenier and Lisa Mastrangelo (2004). Winner of the WPA Best Book Award for 2004–2005.
Rhetorics, Poetics, and Cultures: Refiguring College English Studies (Expanded Edition) by James A. Berlin (2003)

WRITING A PROGRESSIVE PAST

Women Teaching and Writing in the Progressive Era

Lisa Mastrangelo

Parlor Press
Anderson, South Carolina
www.parlorpress.com

Parlor Press LLC, Anderson, South Carolina, USA

© 2012 by Parlor Press
All rights reserved.
Printed in the United States of America

SAN: 254-8879

Library of Congress Cataloging-in-Publication Data

Mastrangelo, Lisa.
  Writing a progressive past : women teaching and writing in the Progressive Era / Lisa Mastrangelo.
     p. cm.
  Includes bibliographical references and index.
  ISBN 978-1-60235-258-2 (pbk. : alk. paper) -- ISBN 978-1-60235-259-9 (hardcover : alk. paper) -- ISBN 978-1-60235-260-5 (adobe ebook) -- ISBN 978-1-60235-261-2 (epub)
 1. English language--Rhetoric--Study and teaching--United States--History--19th century. 2. English language--Rhetoric--Study and teaching--United States--History--20th century. 3. Women authors, American--Education. 4. Women--Education (Higher)--United States--History. 5. American literature--Women authors--History and criticism. 6. Authorship--Social aspects--United States. 7. Women and literature--United States--History--19th century. 8. Women and literature--United States--History--20th century. I. Title.
  PE1405.U6.M37 2012
  810.9'9287071--dc23
                                    2011051701

Cover design by David Blakesley.
Cover image: "OpenGate," 02-11-08 © A-Digit. Used by permission.
Printed on acid-free paper.

Parlor Press, LLC is an independent publisher of scholarly and trade titles in print and multimedia formats. This book is available in paper, cloth and Adobe eBook formats from Parlor Press on the World Wide Web at http://www.parlorpress.com or through online and brick-and-mortar bookstores. For submission information or to find out about Parlor Press publications, write to Parlor Press, 3015 Brackenberry Drive, Anderson, South Carolina, 29621, or email editor@parlorpress.com.

This book is dedicated to the three generations of
women who taught me to love history:
Nain, Mom, and Amy

Contents

Acknowledgments *ix*
Introduction *xi*

1 John Dewey and Progressivism *3*

2 Fred Newton Scott and the Legacy of Deweyian Progressive Writing Instruction *35*

3 Clara Stevens and the Mount Holyoke College English Department *64*

4 Sophie Chantal Hart and Wellesley College *94*

5 Learning from the Past, Looking to the Future *128*

Notes *139*
Works Cited *145*
Index *157*
About the Author *163*

Acknowledgments

It is often said that it takes a village to raise a child; this manuscript has been raised up in much the same way. So many people over the years have been generous enough to lay hands on it. For starters, I would like to thank Dr. Judith Fetterley, Dr. Bob Yagelski, and Dr. Ron Bosco. They had faith in the project from its inception, and saw it through to a dissertation. Victoria Tischio has read many versions of many chapters right from the beginning, and helped me regain faith and focus in the project more than once. Her friendship and her value as a close reader are not to be underestimated.

In the intervening years, so many women in composition and rhetoric have listened to my tales and helped further my thought process. The members of the Coalition of Women Scholars in the History of Composition and Rhetoric are particularly to thank for their ongoing conversation, and their suggestions for looking here or there or thinking or writing here or there. Nan Johnson, Vicki Tolar Burton, Lynee Gaillet, Wendy Sharer, Kate Adams, and Jackie Jones Royster have helped me rethink things time and time again. I am sure many of them do not even realize the impact of their comments, but I remain grateful to them nonetheless.

This project would not be anywhere as complete as it is without the assistance of various archivists in archives across the country. Patricia Albright of the Mount Holyoke archives was one of the first people to assist me in my project, and her input was invaluable. Without her, I would not have explored the work of Clara Stevens, and this manuscript would not exist. Jennifer Gunter King of Mount Holyoke College, Wilma Slaight and Ian Graham of Wellesley College, Karen Jania and the many archivists at the Bentley Historical Library, Craig Simpson and Amanda Remster of Kent State University, Dean Rogers of Vassar, and Eric Hillemann of Carleton College all deserve acknowledgement. I appreciate their willingness to share documents and to respond thoughtfully to inquiries. Without their work, I could not have done my own.

Other scholars over the years have been generous enough to speak with me about their own work, helping further my own. I would like to especially thank Suzanne Bordelon for sharing her work on Gertrude Buck. In addition, Edgar McCormick was generous enough to speak to me about his work on the Emily Wolcott letters, and to point me to their locations in Ohio and New York.

My colleagues at the College of Saint Elizabeth have always encouraged my scholarship and have provided support and feedback at critical times in the process. I owe particular thanks to Kim Grant, Mary Chayko, Margaret Roman, Amira Unver, Laura Winters, and John Marlin.

I would like to especially thank David Blakesley of Parlor Press, who has provided tremendous encouragement and has seen the project through bumps and bruises. In addition, many thanks to Patricia Sullivan and Catherine Hobbs for suggestions and Terra Williams for thoughtful editing.

Barbara L'Eplattenier has lived through this manuscript as both a friend and a scholar. Her ability to make me laugh and to see past setbacks is one that would not be easy to replace. For her encouragement and support of all of the various roads I have been down, I owe her many thanks.

Finally, my family has supported this and me in ways I can never repay. Anthony has lived with these characters as long as I have, and I thank him for his infinite patience. Grace has had no choice but to be involved with this project since her birth. I thank her for understanding that sometimes I have to work, and for reminding me it is equally important to go and play.

Introduction

As I completed graduate work in composition and rhetoric and began my own career as a compositionist at a women's college, I worked to situate myself theoretically and pedagogically within my field. I began to realize more and more that my key interests were in history, and in the stories various histories had to tell me. My graduate work had largely been in the history of composition; I was particularly interested in female composition instructors at the Seven Sisters colleges during the Progressive Era, and it was a heady and exciting time to be doing doctoral work. The kind of history that interested me in the mid-1990s was a relatively new phenomenon in composition and rhetoric. When I began, works like James Berlin's *Rhetoric and Reality: Writing Instruction in American Colleges, 1900–1985* and *Writing Instruction in Nineteenth-Century American Colleges*, Alfred Kitzhaber's *Rhetoric in American Colleges, 1850–1900*, Nan Johnson's *Nineteenth-Century Rhetoric in North America*, and David R. Russell's *Writing in the Academic Disciplines, 1870–1900*, were some of just a small shelf of books available to me that directly addressed the history of the field. Robert Connors's *Composition-Rhetoric* and Sharon Crowley's *Composition in the University* were published as I completed my course work. As I continued to work, however, the revolution grew; books that dealt with the history of composition and rhetoric in general, and alternative sites in particular, were published steadily. The publication of Andrea Lunsford's *Reclaiming Rhetorica: Women in the Rhetorical Tradition*, Louise Wetherbee Phelps and Janet Emig's *Feminine Principles and Women's Experience in American Composition and Rhetoric*, Catherine Hobbs's *Nineteenth-Century Women Learn to Write*, Wendy Sharer's *Vote and Voice: Women's Organizations and Political Literacy, 1915–1930*, David Gold's *Rhetoric at the Margins: Revising the History of Writing Instruction in American Colleges, 1873–1947*, and Jessica Enoch's *Refiguring Rhetorical Education: Women Teaching African American, Native American, and Chicano/a Students,*

1865–1911 all supported my own developing assertion that I was part of a larger (and ever-growing) tradition of scholars who were working on alternative sites of rhetoric and composition.

Scholars in other fields were working to reclaim their progressive roots as well. Linda J. Rynbrandt's *Caroline Bartlett Crane and Progressive Reform: Social Housekeeping as Sociology*, Geraldine Jonçich Clifford's *Lone Voyagers: Academic Women in Coeducational Institutions, 1870–1937*, Ardis Cameron's *Radicals of the Worst Sort: Laboring Women in Lawrence, Massachusetts, 1860–1912*, and Dorothy and Carl Schneider's *American Women in the Progressive Era, 1900–1920* were part of a growing trend of books about women in the Progressive Era that were published in the 1990s. Continued interest in the Progressive Era was evident; in 2002 the *Journal of the Gilded Age and Progressive Era* was first published, indicating enough interest across disciplines for a full journal. Interest in the time period was clearly growing, including my own.

Despite the growth of publications regarding the Progressive Era, however, contextualized Progressive Era history, influences, and pedagogy (including women's pedagogies) were still largely unrepresented as a potential site for scholarship in rhetoric and composition. When I first began this project, I knew a few names of progressive women who had done important things—Jane Addams, Margaret Sanger, Ida Tarbell; however the only progressive female in the history of rhetoric and composition I had ever heard of was Gertrude Buck. The rest of my research unfolded because of a single undocumented sentence from Berlin's *Rhetoric and Reality* regarding Mount Holyoke College's course offerings between 1900 and 1920. While discussing course offerings at colleges around the country, Berlin wrote, "Mount Holyoke even offered an undergraduate major in rhetoric" (56). I remember sharing this sentence with a colleague (a theorist!) who looked me straight in the eye and said "So what?" Nonetheless this piqued my curiosity on two levels—first as a composition historian, and second as a Mount Holyoke alumna. Who was teaching this? What did this look like? I had not realized that there was such a thing as a major in rhetoric dating back that far. Who designed this? My questions led me to the Mount Holyoke archives, where a helpful archivist recommended the papers of Clara Frances Stevens, graduate of Fred Newton Scott's famous rhetoric graduate program in 1894, long-term chair of the Mount Holyoke Rhetoric department, and designer of the rhetoric major. Documents about Stevens revealed a progressive, thoughtful, well-respected teacher who did not fit the Harvard model I was familiar with. In researching Stevens, I came to the conclusion she must not have been alone in her work—other women must have been doing similar work in other locations. Where were the others? While researching women who might have had similar accomplishments in composition, I found Sophie Chantal Hart, long-standing chair of Wellesley's English department and University of Michigan graduate (MA 1898). While I have never seen other references to Stevens in field publications, after some searching, I began to see current references, albeit acontextualized, to Hart. These references appear in such places as Kitzhaber's *Rhetoric in American Colleges, 1850–1900* (although only anonymously in the text—an endnote reveals Hart as his source) (149). Hart also appears in places such as Crowley's *Composition in the University* and John C. Brereton's *The Origins of Composition Studies in the American College, 1875–1925*. More recently, Randall Popken refers to her in his 2004 essay on Edwin Hopkins. All of these texts present or refer to snippets of Hart's single scholarly publication, but make no comment on its author. Who was she?

After much research, I found that both Stevens and Hart had rich histories as teachers, members of their college communities, and scholars. Ultimately, I discovered many connections between the two, including lengthy chair-ship of their own departments. They were also both working from the progressivist tradition John Dewey had started and implemented so broadly, which means they shared many philosophical and pedagogical values. Both completed graduate work at the University of Michigan under the guidance of Fred Newton Scott. Neither published heavily during their lifetime, and each devoted their energies primarily to teaching and to researching and critiquing the teaching of writing. I experienced the thrill of archival research on the day I discovered Hart and Stevens had indeed met. A transcription of a conference session revealed a conversation that involved both of them as they discussed the methods of writing instruction employed in their Progressive Era classrooms.[1] Researching Stevens and Hart offered me a glimpse into the history of Deweyian progressive pedagogy in the writing classroom through the lens of women's education. What struck me most in my research about Stevens and Hart were the methods they employed in teaching writing. This became a major focus for me: Attempting to recover the work of both and place it within a

Deweyian progressive tradition can help current composition instructors understand the roots of their field as well as offer a picture of this type of progressive education that is rarely seen.

Stevens and Hart taught composition in a field that was, as were all academic fields at that time, just developing and male-dominated. They also engaged in what can now be labeled progressive practices in their teaching, implementing Deweyian pedagogy and searching for ways to expand on it. In many ways, they had ample opportunity to do such things. While women's colleges were controversial from an outsider's point of view, they were also relatively unsupervised. Little attention seems to have been paid to what went on in the actual classroom practices of teachers. While course descriptions and content might provoke controversy (whether women should be allowed to learn languages reserved for religious studies students, for example), actual classroom practices seem to have gone relatively unobserved. Consequently, women could focus on experimental and progressive methods of teaching without fear of reprobation. In the case of both Stevens and Hart, they were fortunate enough to have the trust of the department chair and the president (or Principal) of the school. In both cases, the president relied primarily on department chairs to oversee their faculty. However, in both cases, the department chairs in turn relinquished full authority to their instructors. As a result of this combination of factors, Hart and Stevens were able to involve themselves in progressive pedagogy and the instruction of composition with little outside resistance, later themselves becoming department chairpersons who could advocate for such methods.

The time period and location of Stevens's and Hart's work were very important to what they did and how they did it. Both Hart and Stevens were working at eastern women's colleges (the Seven Sisters in particular), and both were students of Deweyian progressive pedagogy, an approach that, among other things, views students as active learners on an experiential continuum. I, of course, was aware of none of this background as I began researching them. I had to start with basic (and confusing) definitions of what it meant to be teaching during the Progressive Era (1880–1920). As Daniel Rodgers confirms in "In Search of Progressivism," scholars right into the 1980s have not been able to agree on a clear definition of the Progressive Era, and often their attempts to create lists of dominant characteristics of Progressive Era theory wind up contradicting themselves. Rodgers observes that the Progressive Era was "an era of shifting, ideologically fluid, issue-focused coalitions, all competing for the reshaping of American society" (114). One of these issues was, of course, education. In addition, social reform, bureaucracy, and industrialism all competed for attention from progressives. Changes in society at this time included an increase in immigrant populations, the development of industrialization, continued geographic expansion, and a perceived need to control such burgeoning enterprises as government and education. Instead of coming up with a list of common goals, Rodgers asserts that progressivism had "three distinct social languages—to articulate their discontents and their social visions. To put rough but serviceable labels on those three languages of discontent, the first was the rhetoric of antimonopolism, the second was an emphasis on social bonds and the social nature of human beings, and the third was the language of social efficiency" (123). Of these, my greatest interest was on education and the emphasis of social bonds that seemed to be so prevalent in the teachers I was exploring.

The person who had been the United States' greatest advocate for examining social bonds and this impact on the educational process was John Dewey. Dewey believed the school functioned as a smaller version of the community itself, and could therefore be a locus for changing all social problems (Sproule 11). The more I began to read about the Progressive Era in general and Dewey in particular, the more I came to see just how influential these theories had been on his friend and colleague, Fred Newton Scott, and in turn on teachers like Stevens and Hart. I began to see that I was looking at a chronology and a genealogy—one that began with Dewey and his general theories, moved to Fred Newton Scott and his theories about rhetoric and the teaching of writing, and then continued on to the teachers Fred Newton Scott had so significantly influenced.

Because of its importance, in addition to recovering Hart and Stevens as writing instructors, another main focus of this project is the recovery of rhetorical instruction during the Progressive Era itself. While many accounts of the history of writing instruction discuss this time period (1880–1920), very few scholars actually situate the events of their composition histories within the Progressive Movement. Russell's *Writing in the Academic Disciplines* and Katherine Adams's *Progressive Politics and the Training of America's Persuaders* are two of the few texts that discuss the historical context of the Progressive Era and the ways it affected the practice of writing. When viewed in conjunction with one another, the history of Stevens and Hart, combined with the history of Dewey and Scott and scholars like Gertrude Buck, allows today's composition scholars to see that both Deweyian and feminist progressive pedagogies have been an integral presence in our tradition even earlier and more extensively than is usually recognized. If we are to fully understand the implications of writing instruction at this time, it seems imperative to embed the instruction that was being given in its full history. As a result, I read widely about the Progressive Era in sources from other disciplines, including history and sociology. In addition, I worked with general sources on progressivism in order to develop as complete a picture as possible of the work Hart and Stevens were doing at this time.

Because of the nature of progressivism, reiterating the ways it has influenced collegiate education was vital to this book. It has been difficult to extricate competing theories and their followers, but clear divisions eventually arose for me between administrative progressives (sometimes called "traditionalists") and Deweyian progressives, which I discuss in the first chapter. The work of Fred Newton Scott (discussed at length in Chapter 2), the most important and influential Deweyian compositionist of the Progressive Era, was much easier to locate. Scott published prolifically and much has been published about him. It was not as easy, however, to find in-depth information about the teachers he influenced. Recovering Stevens and Hart had its own difficulties, some more challenging than others. Stevens published three scholarly articles in her lifetime; Hart published two articles about teaching writing as well, but only one in a scholarly journal (the second appearing in Wellesley's *Alumnae Quarterly*). Her other publications, in *Association of Collegiate Alumnae* and *Home Progress*, do not focus on the teaching of English. As a result, Stevens's and Hart's pedagogies and their administrative work must be pieced together using these short pieces of scholarship combined with archival records of department meetings, memorials written by students who studied with them, and other unofficial documents.

Clearly, much of the work I did was based on archival research. As Rynbrandt mentions of her archival work on sociologist Caroline Barlett Crane, archives contain information that is "arbitrary, uneven, and fragmentary" (12), making archival research more complex than traditional research. As well, there are Foucaultian difficulties with knowledge and power, "due to the imbalance of power between archivist and researcher, the restricted access to knowledge and the complete, constant surveillance exercised over the researcher during the use of archival material" (12). Even what gets kept of the detritus of previous lives often seems arbitrary.

Archival records also have their own idiosyncrasies. Many of Wellesley's early records were destroyed by fire, leaving little to work with. While Mount Holyoke's early collection is more complete, I still encountered other problems peculiar to archival work. Archivist Patricia Albright and I struggled for an afternoon to figure out how Clara Stevens could have signed and submitted an alumnae form *after* her death, finally to discover that her sister (another Mount Holyoke faculty member) seems to have signed the form for her.

But scholarship based on so few official documents (even archival ones) has its risks. It is difficult to avoid putting words into the mouths of both women. At the same time that I wanted to speak honestly for both of them, I also wanted them to conform to my argument. There is danger, of course, in speaking *for* them. In doing this kind of research, in reviving these women's voices, I also had to acknowledge the complexities involved. I had to recognize the contradictions in the positions both women take on writing instruction and work to make those contradictions clear rather than merely trying to resolve them. Both women are already located in contradictory positions: both worked to maintain their positions as professors during a time when constructions of women as mothers prevailed, and both were teachers in a Deweyian progressive tradition where current-traditional models were aggressively advocated for and largely dominant.

The recovery of the Progressive Era as a politically charged, educationally-centered period helps to increase our understanding of the changes in writing instruction and the reactions to them. Mere recovery, however, as scholars such as Patricia Bizzell and Bruce Herzberg have pointed out, is not enough. It is what is done with the recovery and the ways it is interpreted and made available for future use that becomes important. It is through my research regarding Stevens and Hart that I have come to better understand my own place as a female (and feminist) composition instructor in the academy. This is, in addition to being an archival project, an inherently feminist project. I don't just say this because it involves the recovery of two women and their practices, but because I take a feminist stance in doing so. I am participating in what Gesa E. Kirsch and Jacqueline Jones Royster define as a feminist rhetorical practice, where

> feminist rhetorical scholars are actively engaging in the push in the field toward better informed perspectives of rhetoric and writing as a global enterprise, addressing various practices in other geographical locations through feminist informed lenses; [and] rescuing, recovering, and inscribing women rhetors both distinctively in locations around the world and in terms of the connections and inter-connections of their performances across national boundaries. (646)

It is also feminist because it challenges and expands our current histories, and places women in a movement now often seen as feminist (progressivism) (Lebsock 36; Rynbrandt 59). Scholars such as Suzanne Lebsock and Rynbrandt define progressivism as a women's movement, regardless of the fact that women had "little formal political power" (Rynbrandt 59). It is difficult, therefore, to extricate feminism and progressivism. According to J. Stanley Lemons, "at the end of the century the feminist movement became part of the agglomeration called the Progressive Movement; and the various elements cut across, reinforced, and promoted each other" (ix). Likewise, James Livingston, using the term "pragmatism," a slightly earlier philosophy from which progressivism was derived, also points out that the two movements cannot be seen as mutually exclusive or inclusive of each other.[2] "Feminism incorporates what pragmatism initiates, but [...] pragmatism itself is unlikely if not inconceivable in the absence of feminism" (7). Livingston argues that the two are on an "intellectual continuum that begins with pragmatism and ends (for the time being) with feminism" (7). But it is also important to remember that the two began at very similar times (first wave feminism is somewhat earlier than pragmatism, and pragmatism does not seem to have experienced a rebirth the way feminism did). As such, they were influential to one another and therefore are difficult to separate. In participating in feminist historiography, I also view these women as complex and even contradictory players in a particular sociohistorical movement, as well as place them as progressive and innovative female teachers of rhetoric, teaching an all-female population. Lastly, I participate in adding "to the expanding feminist sociohistorical discourse which, in part, uncovers the silences of the past" (Rynbrandt 15).

Some may question my claim that I am looking at alternative sites of rhetorical theory given that much work has already been done on elite, private, eastern women's colleges and that they represent the elite and dominant story of composition history. While it is true there has been substantial work on the history of women's colleges, especially the Seven Sisters, my in-depth work with archival documents specifically investigating the teaching of rhetoric shows that while administration often represented themselves as antithetical to women's public expression and education to be full participants in civic discourse, professors like Clara Stevens and Sophie Chantal Hart reveal this to be anything but true. Overall, the history I present recasts this view of women's education, placing it where it belongs—in a tradition that was largely progressive, sometimes contradictory, but always complex.

Interestingly, Mount Holyoke is typically classified as an elite college, and yet study shows that the majority of her students during the Progressive Era were from middle-class families, rather than the wealthy elite who typically attended Wellesley College. According to David F. Allmendinger, Mount Holyoke students typically came from families of modest means and the college "did not arise from impulses within a wealthy elite, nor did it function primarily to serve that elite" (31). Merle Curti takes this even further, noting that one of Mary Lyon's main purposes in founding Mount Holyoke was "to break the monopoly the upper classes had enjoyed in educating their daughters: her institution was frankly intended to make possible an education for the middle classes" (174). Yet this history of Mount Holyoke does not seem to have filtered down through rhetoric and composition histories. Regardless of the economic circumstances of the students, by 1880–1920, the instruction was progressive. Even the more wealthy students at Wellesley were still taught by progressives rather than conservatives in most subjects (it would be difficult, for example, to be more radical than socialist English Literature professor Vida Scudder, who has her own FBI file). This progressivism in women's colleges, however, has not typically been highlighted by scholars; nor has its relationship to the teaching of rhetoric. Yet my work fits into the work other Progressive Era scholars have completed. As David Gold comments about the sites he explored (Wiley College, Texas Woman's University, and East Texas Normal College),

> English instructors stressed the rhetorical components of writing; introduced politics and discourses of power into the class-

room; encouraged both self-expression and participation in public discourse; took great personal interest in their students' emotional, academic, and social development; and tried to develop dynamic, useful, locally responsive classroom methods and materials. They introduced innovative pedagogies such as peer review, student grading, portfolios, proposal arguments, and group work. (4)

Gold might as well have been describing the work at Mount Holyoke and Wellesley, although he criticizes both of these schools (wrongly) based on early scholarship on the rhetorical programs at the two institutions (65). Likewise, when he discusses Wiley College, a small, black, liberal arts college in Texas, he describes the curriculum as having a complex literary program with a strong oral component:

> In the early 1920s, [Wiley] also had a debating club, which met weekly for intracampus discussions and debates, and a department of expression, which offered classes in essentials of public speaking, argumentation and debate, and interpretation of dramatic literature; for several years, debating was required of all students. In addition to classes in public speaking, public speaking was integrated into freshman English studies; students studied both 'written and oral expression' and were required 'to make several formal addresses before the class' (*Catalog 1920* 37) in addition to writing daily themes. (25)

The curriculum at Mount Holyoke and Wellesley, however, are remarkably similar to what Gold describes. It is clear, then, that both Mount Holyoke and Wellesley were participating in a tradition that was much closer to progressive colleges such as Wiley rather than traditional ones such as Harvard, and yet the histories have consistently shown them in a more traditional light.

Ultimately, the question of whether or not materials no one has explored have value must be raised. Obviously, I believe there is much value in what can be found in archival records, sporadic publications, and department notebooks regarding the teaching of composition. That, in turn, can aid and assist contemporary composition professors, many of whom still feel they are working without recognition and without a lineage. As Gold astutely observes, history matters, even if it is incomplete (152). This history of writing instruction at Mount

Holyoke and Wellesley helps inform and create our current practices. According to Gold, "the perceived pedagogical failures and successes of the past and present shape the pedagogy of the future" (152). Simply providing a revised history is not enough, but it is a start. Critical awareness and careful interpretation of that history will (and should) follow in order to fully understand that what composition instructors see today as progressive or feminist has a history, has a reason, and has been tested before. As Kirsch and Royster advise, we need to continue to do "rescue, recovery, and (re)inscription" work, but we must do more than that as well (647). Whether or not composition will be able to continue its move toward professionalization (although institutional support is not always a given) is questionable. With continued work to recover a previously unexplored past, however, composition instructors can not only learn from the past but can use that past to place themselves within a tradition.

In an effort to move beyond rescue, recovery, and reinscription, this manuscript uses Royster and Kirsch's model for excellence in feminist rhetoric studies as a framework, engaging in what they call "critical imagination, strategic contemplation, and social circulation" (648). Critical imagination is especially pertinent when working with archival documents such as the ones presented here. It asks researchers to gather the available evidence and "think between, above, around, and beyond this evidence to speculate methodically about probabilities, i.e., what might likely be true based on what we have in hand…[and] interrogating the contexts, conditions, lives, and practices of women who are no longer alive to speak directly on their own behalf" (650). This framework allows me to move beyond simple recovery in an attempt to see these women in their own sociohistorical frameworks, as well as developing connections to my own beliefs and practices. Combined with strategic contemplation (my ability to imagine beyond what the documents show and tell me) and social circulation (understanding the overlapping sociocultural circumstances that informed these women's lives), this framework provides a rich and thick theoretical basis for my project. It also allows me to name and articulate my stance toward these women.

Many people throughout the course of this book have asked me why I am personally so interested in recovering the work of these two women and repositioning them within a progressive tradition. The answer lies in the effects of history on knowledge and its connections to subject positions in general. In much the same way I am interested in knowing about my ancestors as a way of positioning and understanding myself, I am also interested in historical recovery in composition as a way of seeing or understanding a more complex picture of the field than has previously been developed. The history of women's education has received more attention in recent years, and yet writing instruction at places such as small, private women's colleges has largely been unexplored. Nor has the Progressive Era as a time period that directly affected that instruction. As a result, an under-history that is largely unknown has consequently been overlooked. It is important to note, though, that while the work of teachers like Stevens and Hart is of the utmost importance in beginning to rewrite the history of composition studies, to say they were anomalous and claim them as *extraordinary* women, as Gail B. Griffin points out, continues to keep the history of women as a whole enshrouded in the dark (31). They were certainly not alone as progressive scholars. While they are two examples, they are two examples of many, most of which have yet to be rediscovered. As my research unfolded, I began to see other women, other progressive instructors, linked to one another and to progressive education as a whole. While I have only explored two of them here, Stevens and Hart are representative of a much larger body. According to Gold, "such small-scale local histories can illuminate, inform, challenge, and inspire larger histories" (7). They can also complement them, working to create a complex, diverse, and rich history. Stevens and Hart represent a piece of a story rather than the story itself.

Not everyone, of course, remains convinced of the value of a history such as this one. When I first began this project, I wrote a paper about the program at Mount Holyoke College and about Clara Stevens for a History of Rhetoric course I was taking. The professor's only comment at the end of the paper was "An interesting historical perspective—although I think that you have to work pretty hard to show convincingly that gender has had an institutional role in shaping views of rhetoric and composition." I always found this comment ironic, in no small part because the paper was later published in *Rhetoric Review* and thus credited as scholarly and informative (Mastrangelo, "Learning from the Past"). But his view has convinced me all the more of the need for work such as this, taken on in recent years by scholars such as Katherine Adams, Wendy Sharer, Joy Ritchie and Kate Ronald, Suzanne Bordelon, Susan Jarratt, Shirley Wilson Logan, David Gold,

Jessica Enoch, and Cheryl Glenn, to name just a few. This very work helps prove that gender indeed has had an influence on the history and the development of the discipline in profound ways, and that we have much still to learn from such a history.

It is important to think about our past as we think about our future in composition studies. As a composition instructor, I am constantly aware of the rich history of rhetorical instruction that precedes my place in the academy. Imagining these woman teaching at the turn-of-the century, standing in front of their classes, figuring out how to best teach the women they were charged with, I feel a connection to my own experiences. I was one of those women in college. I now teach writing at a women's college. I now stand in front of my classrooms and wonder how best to teach my students. As the field becomes more and more professionalized, and as more and more scholarship appears on innovative and progressive ways to teach students how to write better, it is important to understand there is no need to reinvent the wheel. Rather, we should look to our past, and to Deweyian pedagogues like Sophie Chantal Hart and Clara Frances Stevens, who can teach us much through their examples, if only we can invoke critical imaginings of them.

WRITING A PROGRESSIVE PAST

1 John Dewey and Progressivism

No experience is educative that does not tend both to knowledge of more facts and entertaining of more ideas and to a better, a more orderly, arrangement of them.

— John Dewey

The object of education is social improvement. Education is really needed for the purpose of making better citizens. This is practically the same thing as the higher end, social progress, which we saw to be the condition to increase human happiness. If education cannot accomplish this end, it is worth nothing.

—Lester Frank Ward

In developing a critical imagination with a subject, it is vital to understand the context in which my research subjects lived and worked. As Kirsch and Royster ask, "How do we transport ourselves back to the time and context in which they lived, knowing full well that it is not possible to see things from their vantage point?" (648). While we cannot recreate their vantage point, in order to try to understand it with greater clarity it is important to foreground my discussion of Sophie Chantal Hart and Clara Stevens with a conversation about progressivism, and in particular, progressive teaching practices. Particularly because progressivism is so difficult to define, any discussion of progressive teaching practices must be framed with a discussion of the different types of progressivism and their importance to my argument. Doing so allows me to better situate myself critically with my material and to create a more complex picture of it.

The Progressive Era is a rich and vital time to critically imagine. In the late nineteenth century, as part of the Progressive Movement, education through schooling was touted as a powerful method for curing social ills. In addition to the establishment of public schools, social conditions, especially those of the poor, were scrutinized. With its focus on education and social programs, the importance of progressivism was solidified in the 1890s, when it became more of a movement rather than isolated efforts on the part of various politicians and educators (Rodgers 117).[1] According to Derrick P. Alridge, "progressives believed that humans were innately good and kind, and that social reform, not revolution or a complete overhaul of society, was the best means to improve American society" (423). Publications such as Jacob Riis's *How the Other Half Lives* in 1890 brought about a more heightened awareness of the substandard social and economic conditions of many of the immigrants in the United States. Foundations and settlements for the poor were started, as were vocational and educational programs intended to help immigrants and other poor workers gain skills. Such settlements sponsored a variety of programs including medical care centers, day nurseries, and playgrounds (Cremin 16). Perhaps the most famous and well remembered of the programs was Hull House, founded by Jane Addams and Ellen Gates Starr in 1889 in Chicago. According to *Pedagogies of Resistance: Women Educator Activists, 1880–1960*, Hull House, like Toynbee Hall in London, the Henry Street Settlement in New York, and others around the United States, was "involved in urban investigation, social work, education, politics, public health, the status of women, industrial reform, labor relations, international relations, and the arts" (Crocco, Munro, and Weiler 24). Immigrants at settlements such as Hull House were also encouraged to learn English in order to both advance themselves and to assimilate into American culture. Vocational programs were offered in order to educate children who would later help their parents. Ultimately, one primary focus of progressivist efforts such as Hull House was education, which was seen as the solution to developing a wealthier, highly skilled, literate population (Cremin 42; Bowles and Gintis 19).

Educational progressivism had its roots in earlier educational movements, particularly with reformers such as Johann Pestalozzi and Johann Friedrich Herbart. Pestalozzi, a Swiss-born educator (1746–1827), was best known for his experimental, inclusive, and active methods of teaching. Basing his methods on Jean-Jacques Rousseau, Pestalozzi's technique was consistent with that of the later American Progressive Era in several ways. First, his methods were aimed at social reforms and "an improvement of the social condition of the lower classes through industrial education" (Hughes and Schultz 184). As well, like Dewey after him, Pestalozzi advocated a method of teaching that included connection. He did not, for example, believe in teaching children "words and phrases that they did not understand, and insisted on the substitution of firsthand experience with natural objects as the fundamental starting point of instruction" (Hughes and Schultz 184). Pestalozzi directly addressed writing instruction, having students use slates instead of pen and paper so that they could make corrections and revisions as many times as necessary (Gold 118). Like Dewey after him, Pestalozzi's system of learning was based on "sense impression, knowledge obtained directly through observation, experimentation, and experience" (Gold 118). Teachers, under this model, worked as facilitators.

Likewise, German philosopher Herbart (1766–1814) developed a psychology of learning based on connected experiences. "All human concepts or ideas, Herbart maintained, are the result of human perception of the environment and the attempt to find relationships and differences between the phenomena of experience" (Hughes and Schultz 188). Such connections would later play a significant role in progressive education in the United States. The use of Pestalozzian and Herbartian methods appeared in the United States in the middle of the nineteenth-century. Edward A. Sheldon of Oswego, New York, is typically credited with introducing Pestalozzi's methods in the United States around 1860. James Monroe Hughes and Frederick Schultz observe that by 1880, the "'Oswego movement' had completely reshaped instruction in the better elementary schools throughout America" (185). Eventually, this model, combined with the larger social and educational shifts in the United States, resulted in changes in college level instruction as well. Thomas Woody notes that the influence of Pestalozzi and other educational reformers also affected women's education, and more emphasis was placed on academic study. The view that "women must be prepared for 'life,' not simply for 'society'" fueled the seminary and later the collegiate movements (193). In a rupture from Victorianism, women moved out of the home to become more involved in education (including higher education), politics, and social reform (Alridge 424).

Eventually, progressivism came to be commonly associated with education in the United States in multiple disciplines. As Samuel Bowles and Herbert Gintis note in *Schooling in Capitalist America*, the liberal educational theories of progressivists at this time had three goals for education. "First and foremost, schools must help integrate youth into the various occupational, political, familial and other adult roles by an expanding economy and a stable policy" (21). Second, while inequality was seen as inevitable, each individual in a society should be given an equal chance, via education, to compete for the social and economic privileges available. Dewey, for example, exceeded this goal when he advocated for the idea that education should in itself be an equalizing force against inequality and poverty (Bowles and Gintis 21). The third goal of progressive education was that "education is seen as a major instrument in promoting the psychic and moral development of the individual" (21). All three of these goals were fashioned in direct response to the prevailing social conditions in the United States and the perceived need for an increase in education.

Along with theoretical changes and developments in education, progressivism was made possible in the first place by the changes in the industrial and political systems that resulted in the emergence of the notion that all citizens within the democracy had the right to a public education. According to Lawrence Cremin, in *The Transformation of the School*, notions of public education and progressivism played out in the following ways:

> First, it meant broadening the program and function of the school to include direct concern for health, vocation, and the quality of family and community life.
>
> Second, it meant applying in the classroom the pedagogical principles derived from new scientific research in psychology and the social sciences.
>
> Third, it meant tailoring instruction more and more to the different kinds and classes of children who were being brought within the purview of the school. (viii–ix)

With these goals in mind public schools had been founded in every state in America by 1860 (13). In addition, the development of the studies of psychology and sociology, especially facets that concentrated on the learning process of children and the evolution of people as learners, aided progressivism by exploring notions of knowledge acquisition in a democratic school system (Cremin 205). Schools at the elementary and secondary levels continued to grow and develop, and college-level instruction was made increasingly accessible, in part due to the Morrill Land Grant Act of 1862, which allowed states to sell public lands and use the funds for developing public colleges and universities (Crowley 54). The development of teacher training and general pedagogy programs at the college level was in turn fueled in part by the continued standardization of education and the increased need for trained elementary and high school teachers.

John Dewey, the most prominent American advocate for progressive education, believed fully in all of the goals of progressivism (both broad and educational) listed above, and in some cases his pragmatist views even exceeded them. He was a tireless advocate for this type of progressivism, an approach I call *Deweyian progressivism* in order to distinguish it from competing models of the time.[2] While a discussion of Deweyian progressivism is important for setting the context for the rest of this book, it is also important to understand that Deweyian progressivism was never the dominant model for education (including writing instruction) in the United States. In order to contextualize its position, it is therefore necessary to first discuss the two ultimately dominant educational theories from this time: administrative progressivism and current-traditionalism.

MODEL NUMBER ONE: ADMINISTRATIVE PROGRESSIVISM

While the Progressive Movement as a whole took root throughout the United States, a particular branch of it called administrative progressivism evolved with a focus on education. Administrative progressivism and Deweyian progressivism had many shared goals, but few shared methods. Administrative progressivism is, ironically, not particularly progressive but is instead a form of progressivism pioneered and carried out by administrators. This movement developed out of the country's growing sentiment that all citizens should be literate, all should know English, and all should be aware of the social and behavioral norms expected of them as members of the democracy. The goal, then, was "to match these differences in the ability of individual students with the different mental requirements of the vast array of occupational roles required by a complex industrial society" (Labaree 281–2). Administrative progressives were therefore in charge of the implementation and administration of specific programs that sought to cure the nation's high rate of illiteracy and lack of conformity to socialization and dominant behavioral norms. As David Tyack and

Larry Cuban astutely observe, administrative progressives "shared a common faith in educational science and in lifting education 'above politics' so that experts could make the crucial decisions. [. . .] They shaped the agenda and implementation of school reform more powerfully from 1900 to 1950 than any other group has done before or since" (17). Administrative progressives wanted to educate students to standards set by those who were, as the term implies, administrative employees rather than teachers. Administrative progressivism took hold most strongly in elementary and secondary schools, although it did influence collegiate level education as well.

Administrative progressives saw educating students in a standardized curriculum at younger and younger ages as a method of coping with class issues and increasing numbers of immigrants. While cultural diversity was of interest to American citizens, assimilation into the culture was the goal of administrative progressives. David Labaree critiques this practice as "forcing [students] to spend their time in schools becoming socialized for the adult social roles they will play" (283). This socialization was at the expense of individualism. At the same time that education was offered for all, it also was a way of socializing all students into a particular model of behavior, creating a real contrast to the approach of Deweyian progressivism (Bowles and Gintis 23). This ensured that the country had an English-speaking population who were, most importantly, well-versed in the rules and cultural norms of the country. As Tyack and Cuban point out, "educational leaders have tried to transform immigrant newcomers and other 'outsiders' into individuals who matched their idealized image of what an 'American' should be . . ." (2). Primary and secondary education functioned under the premise that all children in America deserved to receive an education (a relatively new democratic notion in the nation's overall history), and began to develop standardized and highly directed methods for educating larger numbers of students within a unified curriculum. Administrative progressives also made it their goal to educate more and more students to higher standards, and this included the increasing population of college students (Berlin, *Rhetoric and Reality* 58). The notion of set standards was itself relatively new and was seen as a progressive move. With all the changes occurring in American society and in academics in the mid-1800s, conditions were right for those who wanted to govern the new system of education.

Administrative progressives often identified with a group Fred N. Kerlinger calls "traditionalists." In a 1958 study of traditionalists, Kerlinger found them more likely to agree with statements that support administrative progressivism, such as "Schools of today are neglecting the three Rs" and "Children need and should have more supervision and discipline than they usually get" (86). These views were in direct contrast with those of a more Deweyian persuasion, who were more likely to agree with statements such as "Education is not so much about imparting knowledge as it is encouraging and prompting the child to use his potentialities for learning" and "True discipline springs from interest, motivation, and involvement in live problems" (86). Such views, Kerlinger found, influenced pedagogical techniques and overall educational theory in individuals (91). While Kerlinger's study was conducted nearly forty years after the typical end of the Progressive Era, it is clear that administrative progressivist notions of learning were still strongly embedded among certain populations.

Administrative progressivism became the dominant model for education in the United States, in large part because administrative progressives focused on exactly that: administration. They were involved in multiple layers of administrative decision making including curriculum, policy, and educational research. In contrast to progressive pedagogues in the classroom, as Labaree asserts, administrative progressives' "focus on the management of schools and the structure of the curriculum gave them an important power advantage over the pedagogical progressives, who focused on teachers and their practice in the classroom" (285). Administrative progressives were thus uniquely positioned to implement their own vision of education. In order to continue to move schools in the directions indicated by administrative progressivists, different teaching methods were required. New methods implemented by administrative progressivists included standardized tests, a unified curriculum (particularly in American history), and a disregard for individual student experience in favor of common experiences. The ultimate goals were social assimilation and the production of a "hybrid but uniform" American (Tyack and Cuban 233). In response, public school teachers in particular searched for consistent ways to teach patriotism, civics, and American history. In an effort to achieve these goals, they taught flag rituals and held nationalistic ceremonies. Approaches such as standardized curriculum and testing were common in part because of the disparate nature of the students' prior experiences; teachers could not assume that students had shared knowledge of skills or attitudes (Tyack 231). Administrative progressives also argued for specialization and disciplinary formation, creating discrete subject areas where generalism used to suffice. College students were also subjected to standardized assignments and tests, page limits, and grading rubrics. Tests measured, in discrete and concrete terms, the so-called progress student learners were making. Such testing was not limited to history or science, however. According to Russell, administrative progressives even saw writing as a "generalizable skill, independent of disciplinary content and context; thus, the mandated page requirements, the error counting, the papers graded for 'content' in one class and 'form' in English class" (*Writing in the Academic Disciplines* 146). These new forms of writing instruction were linked to and codependent with another form of academic progressivism known as current-traditionalism.

Model 2: Current-Traditionalism

The current-traditional model of teaching writing, or current-traditional rhetoric, as it is often labeled, was so named by Richard Young in his 1975 essay "Paradigms and Patterns: Needed Research in Rhetorical Invention." This model has been recognized as the principle basis for composition instruction for the past several decades, but was also widely used during the Progressive Era (Hairston 77).[3] Current-traditionalism, however, is not a form of rhetoric but rather a model of instruction based mostly on decontextualized practice. Originally, Young used the term *current-traditional paradigm* to discuss the current status of composition instruction. In "Paradigms and Patterns," he described it as follows: "The overt features . . . are obvious enough: the emphasis on the composed product rather than the composing process; the analysis of discourse into description, narration, exposition, and argument; the strong concern with usage . . . and with style; the preoccupation with the informal essay and research paper; and so on" (31). Young's use of the term implies the *traditional* use of outmoded texts and conventions in *current* composition teaching.[4] The view of the student is that the student is comprised of a stable, coherent self (a liberal humanist approach) and as such, can create stable, coherent text. *Correct* writing, in such a model, is emphasized over the content of the writing (and the process of writing), and this construction of student work devalues student knowledge by devaluing their active role in the process of composing. In general, this construction was in keeping with academic progressivism and supported it.

Current-traditionalism, in many ways, developed during the nineteenth-century when the emphasis on writing instruction and education in general had turned toward educating an ever-increasing number of students in preparation for the work force (Kitzhaber 43–44). Current-traditionalism winnowed down the elements of belletrism and the scores of writing approaches into a usable set of tools that were widely adaptable to a variety of writing courses. In essence, it attempted to standardize writing instruction in such a way as to allow as many students to pass through writing classes in the most efficient way possible and still teach them what they needed to know. It appealed to administrative progressivists in particular; current-traditional methods of writing instruction clearly implemented administrative progressivism's methods. With a focus on testing and methods for measuring student progress, administrative progressivism and current-traditionalism continued to reinforce each other. A scientific and largely medical model was applied to instruction. Remediation was implemented for the first time as well, particularly in language instruction. As Russell notes, faculty "thus did not all teach language, but merely cooperated in finding and isolating those who needed the 'hospital squad,' a remedial class for students deemed deficient in English by their content teachers" ("The Cooperation Movement" 408). Remedial spelling classes, as well as classes in grammar instruction, were seen at institutions across the country, although they are rarely listed in course catalogs.

The teaching of rhetoric, in many ways, needed to change in order to accommodate the changes in the American system of education and in order to cope with the large numbers of students "who needed to be taught how to write, who needed to be taught correctness in writing, who needed to know forms, and who could be run through the system in great numbers" (Connors, *Composition-Rhetoric* 9). Students entering college also needed to be taught the rules and norms of university education, much in the same way elementary and secondary school children were subjected to social and behavioral enculturation. Whereas previously, the majority of men (and the few women) who were privy to higher education were of the elite, the middle class and a growing number of immigrants with varying cultural backgrounds were now gaining access to higher levels of education, including high school. The socialization of such students into a standard way of thinking, writing, and speaking was more effective with a more standardized approach to instruction (Knoblauch and Brannon 33). Administrative progressives therefore met the needs of a changing university system as well as those at elementary and secondary levels.

It is important to remember that all of these changes were implemented at a time when rhetorical studies itself was undergoing tremendous shifts. These are reflected in course catalogs from the time period as departmentalization, growing numbers of students, increased textbook production, and progressive ideas and practices resulted in changes in rhetoric and rhetorical practice. Whereas previously rhetoric might have been a single course, these changes meant the development of rhetoric as its own area of study, and in some cases, as its own department. Studies in grammar, writing (including orthography), spelling, rhetorical theory, and composition all became separate. Some survived as individual courses, and different concentrations within the field developed, devoted to such areas as themes, principles of rhetoric, argumentative composition, briefs, and general composition.

In addition, speech elements such as declamation, debate, and recitation began to find their own places within the curriculum. Speech teachers had begun, between 1880 and 1920, to collectively form associations and autonomous departments, interested in both elocution and debate as well as other facets of public speaking and communication (Keith 35). This was prompted in large part by the 1914 walkout of speech teachers during the annual meeting of the National Council of Teachers of English. Looking for greater disciplinary recognition and their own individualized organizations, speech teachers began the National Association of Academic Teachers of Public Speaking and the *Quarterly Journal of Speech Education* (Smith, D. 455; Keith 33). Some institutions created separate departments of speech; others maintained speech elements within the rhetoric department.[5]

These developments within speech solidified it as its own area of interest, separate from written communication. Speech, according to Berlin, took with it the "appeal to emotion and the will" (*Writing Instruction* 9). In addition, "discourse dealing with imagination was made the concern of the newly developed literature department. The writing course was left to attend to the understanding and reason, deprived of all but the barest emotional content" (9). As a result, writing instruction turned to more business and analytical forms of writing. This was also in keeping with the German, more scientific influences.

Written communication, however, was also affected by the changing student body and changing social practices. In rhetorical education, Hugh Blair, George Campbell, and Richard Whately were early key influences and offered philosophical and belletristic approaches to writing. From 1850 to 1900, however, changes included simpler doctrines that were thought to be easier for students to follow and for teachers to measure. The teaching of grammar also matched more closely with the United States' intention to more closely align its courses of study with the German model, which was more scientific and therefore more easily measured. Belletristic writing was eschewed in favor of more objective observation, and grammar drills were used to measure success (Berlin, *Writing Instruction* 63). Kitzhaber also observes that "few books advanced rhetorical 'systems'; instead, doctrine became simpler, and a more concrete approach appeared in the textbooks" (76). By the end of the century, in many places, rhetorical education was reduced to a narrowly defined set of rules for writing. Blair, Campbell, and Whately were thought to be too abstract for students. As well, other forms of instruction such as grammar drills were far easier to measure and to show progress. As Connors notes, "college students could not write (the reasoning went), because their early grammar lessons had not 'taken.'" (*Composition-Rhetoric* 129). In reality, changes in educational methods and scores of reports produced by non-academics had more to do with the perceived failure of writing instruction. However, the perception continued to fuel the idea that a current-traditional model of writing instruction would help solve the problems.

The history of the implementation of the current-traditional model in college level writing instruction is well known to most scholars and historians of composition-rhetoric. Historically, Harvard's history of writing instruction provides the most cited and well known (and vilified) example of the current-traditional models. While this history is detailed in depth by scholars elsewhere (see Connors, Crowley, Miller, etc.), it bears summarizing here in order to set the context for the development of progressive education for the simple fact that it provides the basis for the formation of modern composition studies as a whole. In the 1870s, Harvard decided testing, the method the new German model of study supported because it was considered a more scientific measuring device than individual assessment, should be used to measure their students' abilities. Much to their horror, more than half of the Harvard students failed the written exam required after entrance in 1874. The results of this exam were twofold: first, similar exams were adopted for widespread use at colleges across the United States. Second, interpreters of the results announced a literacy crisis among American college students. As Connors notes, "The Harvard exam and the continuing problems students had with it (and with the host of similar writing tests set up by the many colleges that took Harvard for a model in all things) created the first American College Literacy Crisis and the first experiments at basic writing instruction on the college level" (*Composition-Rhetoric* 185). In an effort to solve the *writing problem* and the subsequent embarrassment it caused after the 1870s exam, Harvard began remedial work and insisted on more stringent entrance exams for their own students, who were arguably among the most prepared entering students in the United States. Adams Sherman Hill's English A was implemented in the 1880s as a two-semester course that attempted to separate out those students who were prepared for college writing and those who needed remediation. English A was closest to what is currently known as freshman English. English B (sophomore themes) and English C (junior forensics—a course in argument) were also developed, although these were phased out by the 1890s (Russell, *Writing in the Academic Disciplines* 55). Class sections for English A continually grew in size (classes often contained up to one hundred students) and students wrote prolifically and had their writing critiqued daily; indeed, the 1892 Report of the Committee on Composition and Rhetoric notes that students at Harvard in English A alone were producing over six thousand pieces of writing every semester (Brereton 76). Because of the size of the classes and the volume of writing, papers were typically graded for surface matters instead of content. This allowed instructors to assess large quantities of writing and continued to allow universities to increase class sizes.

The very nature of the three-course sequence at Harvard also encouraged administrative progressivism. Harvard in particular insisted on an interdisciplinary writing program of sorts that placed writing instructors at a unique disadvantage when assessing student papers. Students in English B and English C were required to write from a variety of topics distributed to them. Almost all were taken from other subject matter the students would have studied. While Harvard's early theory of writing across the disciplines seems progressive (and is in keeping with Deweyian theories about connected learning experiences), the subject matters that students were able to write about often forced the writing instructors to continue with current-traditional models of assessment. David R. Russell, in *Writing in the Academic Disciplines, 1870–1990*, cites an excellent example of a student writing for English C. Russell notes that senior Ralph Clinton Larrabee, a future medical researcher, wrote one of his themes on "the algo-fungal theory of lichens." As a result, his writing instructor was nearly unable to evaluate the essay on anything *other* than grammatical issues and superficial correctness. In Larrabee's case, "the instructor's comments betray insecurity: 'Grade A—I find no difficulty in following your argument, which considering the difficulty of the subject is from a layman no small praise'" (55). Harvard's limitation of writing instruction to faculty from a very few disciplines (if there were any outside the English department at all) left instructors little choice but to evaluate on presentation, grammar, spelling, and possibly clarity of argument. While English B and English C were ultimately phased out by the turn of the century, by then instructors were trained and conditioned to evaluate students on matters of superficial correctness (55). Ironically, in 1914 yet another committee found that students' writing skills actually declined after English A. As a result, after this so-called delinquent writers were "handed over to the English department for 'correction'" in another remedial course (called, significantly, English F) (Russell, "The Cooperation Movement" 409). Eventually, skills in composition became the lower, base point on which all students should prove competency. Courses in composition came to mean writing instruction in the most current-traditional way possible—correct grammar, spelling, and usage.

Because courses like English A were administratively motivated, and because so many colleges and universities looked to Harvard as their model, teaching writing after the advent of English A was often narrowly construed. Most instructors used already established models and provided information and topics for the students to write about and carefully corrected essays for grammatical and structural aspects, rather than assessing their content. The use of English A and English F as role models and a dearth of innovative textbooks for teaching them meant teachers saw fewer and fewer possibilities for teaching writing, and it certainly was not seen as an area worthy of intellectual activity and scholarly research. Often, English A was simply used as a required model, restricting teacher input, especially at places that relied heavily on adjunct or part-time labor (Russell, *Writing in the Academic Disciplines* 54). The wide-spread use of English A as a model connected the teaching of writing directly to administrative progressive ideology.

In addition to the perceived 1874 crisis, Harvard published a series of reports between 1892 and 1897 that compounded the evidence of a literacy crisis among student writers entering American colleges. The findings of the Harvard Reports, compiled in 1892, 1895, and 1897 by Charles Francis Adams, E. L. Godkin, and Josiah Quincy (appointed by the Harvard Overseers), espoused grammar instruction and exercises at the elementary and secondary levels as a way to correct the newfound literacy problem. Work at the lower levels, according to the committee, would help reduce the prevalence of remedial work at the college level. Their reports emphasized the need for mechanical correctness, taught through rote memorization and drill.[6] Notably, none of these men had any training or experience in the teaching of writing (Berlin, *Writing Instruction* 61). Their observations were drawn from a combination of short themes written in English A and some entrance exams. Despite this, their recommendations were taken seriously by administrators desperate to maintain standards of excellence at their institutions.

The findings of the committee also seem to imply that the lack of skill in writing was an insult to the function of the college itself. According to Brereton, "the College, consequently, instead of being what its name implies,—a seminary of higher education,—becomes, in thus far, a mere academy, the instructors in which are subjected to the drudgery of teaching the elements" (96). One can see how even the early reports considered the teaching of the basics of composition a mere drudgery, and felt they should be undertaken at some other (presumably earlier) level. Making such a proclamation, however, "thus gave support to the view that has haunted writing classes ever since; learning to write is learning matters of superficial correctness" (Berlin, *Writing Instruction* 61).

There were other reports being compiled as well, providing evidence (much of which claimed to be scientific) of a literacy crisis, particularly at the elementary and secondary levels. The reports of the Committee of Ten, a committee appointed by NCTE in 1892 to investigate the so-called literacy crisis, also placed blame on the secondary schools. This committee was originally charged with helping to design improved curriculum for the secondary schools, so as to alleviate many of the writing problems witnessed at the college level. As Tyack and Cuban note in *Tinkering Towards Utopia: A Century of Public School Reform*, the committee was led by Charles William Eliot of Harvard, and was comprised mostly of "college presidents and professors who wanted to bring some order to the hodgepodge of the high school curriculum, which had come to resemble a species of academic jungle creeper, spreading thickly and quickly in many directions at once" (49). The Committee of Ten wrote their reports solely from an administrative point of view. Their suggestions were based on their findings from reading student papers and they included no consultation with composition instructors, department chairs, or adjuncts. As Sue Carter Simmons observes, the overall conclusions of the reports were "drawn from no direct observation of the work of the instructors, no examination of their students' work, no attendance at their lectures, and no study of the new system of instruction the teachers had recently instituted in the writing courses"—i.e., theme work (332). As a result, much like the evaluation conducted by the earlier three, the evaluation of writing samples by the Committee of Ten looked almost solely at issues such as grammar, usage, spelling, and handwriting.

Throughout these reports, the blame for what was perceived as the illiterate English of college students was often placed squarely on the elementary and secondary schools and their failure to reinforce proper *skills* early on. This view was later adopted by the public as well, largely in response to the reports. As Kitzhaber points out, the reports "used the secondary and preparatory schools as whipping boys, asserting that the colleges had no responsibility in the matter at all. They assumed that the solution of the problem was simple and obvious, and that only the lassitude and ineptness of the lower schools were responsible for the problem's continued existence" (47). While most elementary and secondary school teachers had no training in what we now call composition theory, certainly most were doing a much better job than what the reports might indicate. However, knowing the students would be subjected to entrance exams for schools like Harvard, many teachers began to simply "teach to the test," and to train their students to write the kinds of essays they would need to know. As Fred Newton Scott observes in "What the West Wants in Preparatory English," such an approach disrupted the curriculum, making the senior year of high school a wholly preparatory one. Scott further commented that such an approach consistently forced the teacher to abandon education in favor of preparation and coaching (12).

Harvard was a model to be emulated in the United States at this time and its model of composition spread quickly throughout the colleges and universities in the United States—a rather prestigious claim. As Brereton notes, "Harvard was one of the largest and certainly the most respected of the American colleges [. . .]. Its football team was dominant, its professors were eminent, its president was the most famous educational leader in the nation" (11). It is easy to see, therefore, how its model of composition could spread so quickly and thoroughly. Initially, Harvard became the model for composition in part because of its stature and durability. According to Brereton, "composition had more prestige at Harvard than elsewhere, and its prominence lasted longer" (13). As a result, other colleges looked to Harvard as a model in all things, including composition. In addition, the work at Harvard was publicized heavily through both trade and popular publications. Several of the committee reports were available for public purchase, and reports on composition throughout the country, including at Harvard, were published in the popular journal *The Dial*. Once this series was completed, the vignettes from different colleges and universities were collected and publicly published in 1895, with William Morton Payne as the editor, as *English in American Universities*. The *Atlantic Monthly* also published essays on the ongoing perceived crisis. These included two essays by James Jay Greenough, a Harvard professor, titled "The Present Requirements for Admission to Harvard College" (1892) and "The English Question" (1893), which focused on illiteracy. Kitzhaber notes that Hill also "wrote articles setting forth his views and published them in popular magazines of national circulation" (203).

Field journals also covered the ongoing furor over the new literacy crisis. As early as 1884, in the very first volume of *PMLA* published, author Theodore Hunt lamented the current status of composition studies (in Crowley 59–60). The 1897 January volume of *Educational Review* includes an article by E. L. Godkin, a member of the Schoolmaster's Association of New York, titled "The Illiteracy of American Boys." Godkin's piece was presented to the association as a direct criticism of the Harvard Overseer's Report. In contrast, LeBaron Russell Briggs, a Harvard faculty member, published "The Correction of Bad

English as a Requirement for Admission to Harvard College" in *The Academy* in 1890. While this is just a limited sampling, clearly the issue of the Harvard reports was an important one, to people both in and out of education. Even high schools were aware of Harvard's program and recommendations as they collected required reading lists for students intending to apply (Scott, "Report on the Entrance Exams" 289).

The effects of groups like the Committee of Ten were thus far reaching, and even had implications for the instructors at Harvard. Ironically, college level writing instructors often learned of the results of the reports of the various committees by reading the local newspapers or field journals rather than receiving the information firsthand (Simmons 331). Barrett Wendell, a Harvard instructor, nearly lost his job at one point due to a particularly hostile committee member who had observed the writing of Wendell's students. He felt that Wendell's theme correcting was not up to par, and that his conversational and dialectic methods of evaluation were simply not helping improve student writing (one can only imagine that this particular person wanted to see more grammar drills) (Simmons 340). Such criticism of teaching methods was a common outcome of the reports. As well, because such reports were largely produced by administrative bodies, teachers had few opportunities to publicly respond to them. Responses in field journals often reached the already converted rather than the public at large.

Despite the increased efficiency provided by the Harvard model, not all scholars were convinced of the effectiveness or superiority of it. John Brereton's work explores this issue at length in *The Origins of Composition Studies in the American College, 1875–1925*, which includes over one hundred pages of work by anti-Harvard scholars. This is not to say that all of them were progressive pedagogues; many of them simply felt the methods Harvard was utilizing were poor and should be re-thought. Many thought the teaching of literature should be linked with the teaching of writing, especially as literature and composition became more and more separated, even while still remaining under the auspices of English. Some felt the topics for written material should be expanded to include materials such as magazine and newspaper articles; still others thought the solution "was a 'pure' or 'direct' composition course that emphasized the writer in his or her social relationship . . . rather than [focusing on] the issues of style and correctness that came to dominate the Harvard program" (Brereton 237). While individual articles were published, there was little organized response to any of the attacks on the Harvard program, least of all from Harvard itself. As Brereton notes, Harvard's major theoretical influences actually outlived its program. By the late 1890s, rather than taking time to respond to attacks on its program, Harvard had ultimately lost interest in it and was busy changing it again to a program largely run by adjunct labor. The school was

> scaling back its system, and the only senior faculty involved in composition were those with a special interest in collegiate as opposed to university education, teachers rather than researchers. When they passed from the scene, Harvard's great experiment in composition would be over, and all that remained would be a large first-year writing program staffed by part-time instructors and graduate fellows. (238)

Harvard's immunity to attacks developed in large part from the very fact that so few of its full-time faculty were involved in the writing program by the turn of the century. Adams Sherman Hill, the creator of English A, for example, suffered from ill health and retired by 1904, teaching less and less up until that time (Kitzhaber 62). His three colleagues, Wendell, Baker, and Briggs, also were drawn to other pursuits. Briggs, for example, was appointed the first dean of the Men's College at Harvard in 1891. By 1902 he had become the dean of the faculty of Arts and Sciences. In addition to this and a full teaching load, Briggs became the president of Radcliffe College in 1903 and was appointed the Boylston Professor of Rhetoric and Oratory in 1904, upon Hill's departure (Fley 24). While Briggs (amazingly) continued to teach throughout all of this, his attentions were clearly divided. Baker's attention to the Harvard program was also short-lived. He taught increasingly at Radcliffe, and was also appointed at Wellesley as a visiting professor in 1892 (Hart, *Alumnae Biographical File*). Wendell was perhaps the greatest holdout, although according to Kitzhaber, later in his career he also "abandoned work in composition as an impossible task. Students still wrote badly, and he lamented the years he spent teaching the unteachable" (69). Clearly, while the dedication of these men to intellectual pursuits is obvious, the teaching of freshman composition was not always their first focus. Overall, "faults" later found with the program became the responsibility of already over-burdened graduate fellows, who were most likely in training to become teachers of literature, and adjunct laborers who were (as they continue to be) primarily used for their labor and not usually consulted on matters of major importance to the program such as curriculum design or teaching methods (Brereton 238).

The writing assignments in college classrooms also began to change as a result of the lack of investment of full-time faculty and the continued reports of a literacy crisis (as well as the ensuing recommendations for how to *fix* student error in writing). In many places, themes, instead of functioning as dialectical journal-type entries the professor responded to, had become almost entirely mini-compositions, to be marked and graded according to rubrics instead of individually (a clearly visible difference between an administrative progressive approach and a Deweyian progressive approach). Lecture and recitation format, with very little opportunity for student-teacher interaction, became standard as class sizes became larger. Larger classes meant students were further separated from their instructors (Simmons 330). Often students were subjected to one person who lectured to them, and a second reader (usually an adjunct) who graded their themes. Lastly, attendance in classes at many institutions was voluntary, making it extremely difficult to get to know students even if instructors chose to try (330). Innovations in teaching were also discouraged at many institutions. Consequently, institutional authority usurped any teaching authority and the result was a very narrow conception of the teaching of writing. The effects of such a program have had enormous ramifications for the teaching of writing from then until now.

The methods associated with the Harvard model were not without some merit. On the surface, improving grammar and mechanics seems like a theoretically sound move toward improving student writing overall. However, as Fred Newton Scott himself pointed out in "English Composition as a Mode of Behavior," such methods do not resolve the underlying issues at stake: "I have always held the view, and have frequently expressed it, that a large part of the theme-correcting of which we hear so much complaint, is probably wasted. Not that it fails to secure an immediate reduction of the percentage of error, but that it fails to reach the inward disease of which the errors are merely the outlying and obvious symptoms" (463).[7] As Scott observes, the suggested methods of the reports solved immediate and surface problems; however, they did not alleviate the larger difficulties that lay beneath.

The administrative progressive model actually enabled current-traditional teaching methods in a variety of ways. First, a standardized curriculum was often used to hold all students to the same standards. Standardized testing and assignments also expected the same product, and the emphasis was most often on the product rather than the process. Students were encouraged to be scholarly and to separate their own experiences from their academic work. This model thereby effectively separated writing, thinking, and experience into separate and distinct categories.

Secondly, standardized instruction also allowed teachers the opportunity to respond to students in more efficient and less time-consuming ways. As stated earlier, this efficiency often allowed teachers to simply focus their comments on student error, pointing out places where students needed to fix mistakes. This emphasis on product forced instructors to focus on stylistic matters of writing rather than content. Standardization typically (although not always) excluded emphasis on content and was instead skills-driven, requiring competency in set levels of spelling, grammar, arrangement, and even handwriting.

Thirdly, the students' own sociohistorical backgrounds were generally not considered in programs developed by administrative progressives. Student individuality was curbed in an effort to socialize students into an assimilatory notion of what it meant to be an American student. Current-traditionalism also reinforced this through standardized and preset assignments. Rather than allowing students to design individual assignments, current-traditional approaches instead often emphasized testing student knowledge based on their ability to recall previously taught information, or designed a single assignment for all students in the class to complete. Typically, this assignment would relate to previously taught information and would discourage students from writing about anything personal or making connections to subject matter outside the purview of that particular class. Such teaching methods and assignments did not allow students to make connections between topic information and their own experiences.

While current-traditionalism was particular to writing instruction, its use of administrative progressive methods set it in direct conflict with Deweyian progressivism. As the influences of administrative progressivism continued to create hegemonic models, Deweyian progressivism worked to alter such practices with its overarching focus on the individual and an organic philosophy that focused on connected notions of experience.

JOHN DEWEY AND DEWEYIAN PROGRESSIVISM

Although the pragmatism and progressivism Dewey adopted has influences from much earlier scholars, including Swiss-French novelist Rousseau in the eighteenth century, Swiss educator Pestalozzi in the late eighteenth and early nineteenth centuries, and Horace Mann and Joseph Mayer Rice in the late nineteenth century, its best remembered advocate and scholar in the United States *is* John Dewey. Dewey's primary work in progressivism took place in the first quarter of the twentieth century and blossomed into a movement in early twentieth-century educational theory that focused on active and experiential learning. This form of progressivism, in direct contrast to and competition with administrative progressivism, encouraged self-expression and the development of the individual, working against models that emphasized subject content that might or might not take into account students' sociohistorical and cultural settings. Dewey used tenets of pragmatism, the precursor to progressivism, which constantly involved a world of *transactions*. As Russell Goodman explains, "we do not know things 'in themselves,' but only as intertwined with our contributions of organization, interest, and selection" (2). Experience of any kind, according to Dewey, must be part of what he labeled the "experiential continuum." In other words, "the principle of continuity of experience means that every experience both takes up something from those which have gone before and modifies in some way the quality of those which come after" (*Experience and Education* 35). We create an understanding of our world through these connected experiences. For every experience we have, we compare it to our previous experiences and use those in order to make sense of our world. According to Aaron Schutz, "authentic learning thus happens in the midst of purposeful activity" (269). Dewey's philosophy clearly envisioned a correlation between the student learner and the object of their learning. This transactional theory is linked to the main notion behind Dewey's philosophy—that direct experience of things and analysis of them could lead to a greater understanding of the overall workings of the world around us. Teaching children *about* science (for example, temperature) was passive and would not allow them to see the relationship of science to their own world. Letting them *experience* science for themselves on the other hand (for example, experiencing and comparing hot, mild, and cold temperatures and their effects), would help provide these connections.

In addition, Dewey felt that all subject matter should be directly tailored to the needs and experiences of the students. Students in rural farming areas, for example, would benefit far more from science that emphasized agricultural methods and innovations rather than science that focused on abstract concepts. This was not necessarily because it would train them to become better farmers, but because it would provide them with a context they were more likely to understand and be able to apply to their own learning (*Democracy and Education* 106).

Transforming pragmatism's philosophies for use within the context of progressive education and learning, Dewey added his own theories of active, experiential learning and respect for children as individuals. According to "Progressive Education and the Science of Education," his schools and schools based on his model "[exhibited] a common emphasis upon respect for individuality and for increased freedom; [as well as] a common disposition to build upon the nature and experience of the boys and girls that come to them, instead of imposing from without external subject-matter and standards" (170). Dewey's methods did *not* mean that students were left to their own devices and would not receive any guidance from instructors. To the contrary, he felt that teachers should be guiding forces who helped shape and support student work but did not dictate it (both *Democracy and Education* and *Experience and Education*, among other works, emphasize this). Transaction rather than transmission was the primary form of learning. Through his democratic view and model of teaching and learning, Dewey felt that the school should have an effect on students and students should also affect the school. Dewey saw active forms of education as continuous reflections of experience and influenced his teachers to help students work toward such views.[8]

In his 1938 publication *Experience and Education*, Dewey points out that experience, and connected experience at that, is the most important event in schooling. In *Experience and Education* he notes that the worst mistake that can be made when discussing progressive education is to assume it is a direct opposite of traditional education. Such an analysis would lead people to believe that if experience was important in progressive education, then it was nonexistent in traditional forms of education. Rather, according to Dewey, there is experience in traditional education, but its lack of emphasis is problematic. Dewey states that there are two points that must be included to fully understand his argument. " . . . First, that young people in traditional schools do have experiences; and secondly, that the trouble is not with the absence of experiences, but their defective and wrong character—wrong and defective from the standpoint of connection with further experience" (*Experience and Education* 27). In other words, Dewey's philosophy demanded that teachers not only let students experience more instead of being told about experience but that the experience be connected to others, and form an overall web of experiences. Disciplinary studies, as a result, were troublesome to Dewey, who felt that the collegiate departmentalization of the 1890s and the administrative moves to make subjects (and their coinciding departments) individual and disconnected from other subjects left students without any overall sense of how subjects (and therefore the students' own experiences) related to one another.

Dewey also firmly believed students should be allowed more freedom in the classroom. This is not to say Dewey believed overall control should be relinquished and chaos encouraged. Instead, he felt students should have more control within their own ability to choose and outline various subject matter. By no means did Dewey believe in completely unstructured learning environments;[9] rather, he felt the teacher should not be an authoritarian figure, but instead a more nurturing facilitator who helped the students to have their needs met under appropriate time circumstances. In *Experience and Education*, Dewey utilizes the example of a mother with a newborn infant. "The wise mother takes account of the needs of the infant but not in a way which dispenses with her own responsibility for regulating the objective conditions under which the needs are satisfied" (42). In such a way, teachers should individualize education to take into account student needs, but not to the detriment of the overall classroom experience.

The standardization espoused by administrative progressivism, including the newly developed intelligence testing, was also extremely problematic for Deweyian theory and pedagogy, since it worked against Dewey's views that students should achieve their best potential, not work at a fixed level of learning that might or might not be practically obtainable for the student (or on the other hand, might not challenge the student enough). Any such testing automatically negated the focus on the individual, and also ignored possible strengths students had that would not be accounted for. In Dewey's view, any kind of standardized testing moved too far away from the individual and did not in any way take into account the differing needs and goals of differing students. In "Mediocrity and Individuality," published in 1922, Dewey sums up his views on standardization in the schools:

> we are irretrievably accustomed to thinking in standardized averages. Our economic and political environment leads us to think in terms of classes, aggregates and submerged membership in them. In spite of all our talk about individuality and individualism we have no habit of thinking in terms of distinctive, much less distinctly individualized, qualities. (36)

Dewey's clear focus on the individual had no place in administrative progressivism or current-traditional models of instruction. As a result, Dewey fought an uphill (and ultimately losing) battle for widespread acceptance of his methods and beliefs.

John Dewey and Writing Instruction

While Dewey never wrote specifically about writing instruction, it is not difficult to critically imagine how Dewey's philosophy could be translated for use in the writing classroom at all levels. Many of the key concepts compositionists utilize today, such as active learning, workshopping, and supportive experiential learning, and the very idea that writing, thinking, and experience should be linked, are all part of Dewey's theory of progressivist education and were implemented by many of the men and women teaching writing during the Progressive Era. Stephen M. Fishman is one of the most notable contemporary composition scholars to directly discuss Dewey's philosophies and their relationship to composition instruction, although most current composition scholars and pedagogues are in some way affected by Dewey's work whether they are aware of it or not. In his 1993 article "Explicating Our Tacit Tradition: John Dewey and Composition Studies," Fishman points out the embeddedness of Dewey's philosophy in current composition studies. Fishman observes that one of Dewey's goals is to educate students in such a way that they leave a school or class wanting to know more, as well as wanting to work more with people who were able to contribute to their thinking: "Ideally, Dewey would say, students should leave their composition courses wanting to do more writing. And given his view that we learn best in groups of likeminded people, Dewey would also say students should leave freshman composition [or any other writing course] wanting to do more work in writing groups" (317). Dewey realized no one really works on his or her own, and as a result he advocated for the idea that readers and writers should not and in many ways cannot work in isolation. Since incorporation of other ideas is always present in learning, collaboration results in a wider and broader interactive experience involving one's own work. Composition work, as a result, should encourage students to form writing groups and writing communities, and not to view writing as an individual or individualized process.

Skill-drill testing in any subject, and writing instruction is no exception, also has no place in the Deweyian classroom. In "The Need for a Philosophy of Education," Dewey writes that "the acquisition of skills is not an end in itself. They are things to be put to use, and that use is their contribution to a common and shared life. They are intended, indeed, to make an individual more capable of self-support and of self-respecting independence" (11). Writing then, should be contextualized and any instruction in writing should be seen as building on what had come before, and creating stepping stones for what would come after. In Dewey's *The Middle Works*, he comments that throughout life, there should be "inception, development, fulfillment" (10:62). While she is not referring directly to writing, Charlene Haddock Seigfried explains that Dewey's notion of experience is "organized dynamically, which means that it is characterized by temporality and growth" (145). Growth as a writer, too, is expected; students are not expected to be intellectually static. In this context, Dewey's notions of connected experience also meant condemning standardized writing assignments that excluded students without a *particular* experience, or that did not allow students to make connections from their own experiences (and standardized testing certainly excludes both of those kinds of experiences).[10]

Dewey's "Mediocrity and Individuality" seconds such ideas by discussing the fact that the use of standardized testing ultimately had negative results, pigeonholing students into false categories. Dewey in fact pointed out that this testing was antithetical to democratic practice because such tests were essentially tools for stratification, usually benefiting only those who designed the tests, resulting in the finding of "mediocrities, not individualities" (35). With such a philosophy in mind, endless skill-drill of grammatical structure and rules, without actual writing practice, would have seemed pointless and dangerous to him. In Dewey's mind, skill-drill work in grammar and rules of writing would also be acontextual for the students, not relating in any way to their experience with writing, and would therefore be unproductive and ineffective. Having students work with their own errors and try to correct them, having students work in writing groups with their peers in order to strengthen texts, and encouraging students to study grammar and rules as part and parcel of a more complete writing program would appeal much more to a Deweyian sense of contextuality and related experience than current-traditional, skill-drill based learning.

Ultimately, Dewey's main research and writing was about elementary and secondary school systems. Thus, while Dewey's influence on the structure and character of elementary and secondary education was extremely far-reaching, his philosophy did not have quite the same influence for college level writing instruction. While individual programs and instructors have invoked Deweyian progressive pedagogy as a method in their writing instruction, emphasizing process and connection, overall the dominant model has been one influenced more by current-traditionalism. Dewey did, however, have one follower who truly made a name for himself in the field of composition and rhetoric: Fred Newton Scott, who is discussed in the next chapter.

Dewey and Contemporary Feminist Theories

It is clear that Deweyian pragmatism, progressivism, and nineteenth-century writing instruction have many overt characteristics of what we now call feminist composition theory.[11] His privileging of student experience and voice, links to connected learning and transactional experience, breaking down of binaries, and advocacy for social change are all common goals in feminist thinking, especially in the feminist writing classroom. Linda Markowitz defines feminism as having three main characteristics, all of which are derivative of Dewey: "these are participatory learning, social construction of knowledge and the legitimization of personal experience" (42). Seigfried, in her philosophical explorations of Dewey, also finds strong links between feminist thought and Deweyian pragmatism. As Seigfried points out in *Pragmatism and Feminism*, pragmatism and Deweyian philosophies of education in particular can anachronistically also be called feminist in the sense that women (and men) used such philosophies to work for social change and to protest assigned and rigid social/cultural roles (4). While Progressive Era feminism had its own goals, they were largely used for progressive projects (Lemons ix). As I explore in the following chapters, many women in fact were influenced by and followed Dewey's work and used Dewey's progressivist paradigms, and Dewey consistently (although quietly) credits the women around him for helping to shape his theories. Throughout his life and work, he credits Alice Chipman Dewey (Dewey's wife, and cofounder with him of the Chicago Laboratory School), Ella Flagg Young (first principle of Dewey's Laboratory school), Jane Addams (founder of Hull House), and Elsie Ripley Clapp (a student of Dewey's, and later a teaching assistant of his at Columbia) for influencing his thinking (Seigfried 47–49). As Livingston notes in *Pragmatism, Feminism and Democracy*, there were actually many pragmatist feminists who were working during the Progressive Era. Jane Addams and Jessie Taft, for example, were both working toward feminist goals of social change for women while invoking pragmatist theories (10).

Where, then, do the overlaps occur? Connected experience, so important to Deweyian theory, is certainly a key feature of both. Jane Duran, in "The Intersection of Feminism and Pragmatism," sees connected experience and articulation of that experience as one of the key overlaps between the two. She comments that both feminism and pragmatism privilege "objects-in-their-relations-to-persons; relations and connections become almost more important than particulars themselves, and certainly more important than particulars seen in the detached and distant manner characteristic of androcentric theorizing" (168). Dewey's advocacy of connected experience was absolutely vital to his theory. It also has a clear place in Duran's vision of feminism.

Part of Deweyian connected experience in the classroom also involves having students work in groups in order to create a more supportive classroom environment and help students connect with one another and their subject material. According to Danna L. Walker, Margaretha Geertsema, and Barbara Barnett, "the creation of a participatory classroom community [is] a key principle of feminist pedagogy" (185). Having students work together with the goal of collaborative knowledge formation is a key goal for modern feminist pedagogues. Likewise, having students work together, for Dewey, meant that unique individuals with various experiences could come together to envision and solve problems (Schutz 271). Thus, the idea of participatory pedagogy, like many of the concepts listed here, is both Deweyian and feminist.

In addition, privileging of student voice and disruption of binaries are two areas of composition theory that can be linked to both pragmatism (and, in turn, Deweyian progressivism) and feminism. The privileging of experience and voice is common in feminist composition theory. While Dewey would have seen the expressivist methods of Peter Elbow's *Writing Without Teachers* as going too far toward valuing unexamined and perhaps unconnected personal experience, a more poststructural view of experience is useful to poststructural feminist compositionists and echoes Dewey's theories. *Writer*, in this context, is as much a constructed notion as *woman*. As Chris Weedon describes in *Feminist Practice and Poststructuralist Theory*, the subject in poststructural theory is constantly under construction (i.e., undergoing a constant but ever-changing set of experiences). According to Weedon, language is the location where such construction takes place as it helps us articulate our social reality. This allows language to construct meaning, which does not exist prior to its articulation (40). Understanding this, and understanding that this meaning is socially and historically located within the discourses, can help students to both understand and create meaning through their written work (171). This places students in a very powerful and very Deweyian position of creating meaning through the conceptualizing, connecting, and recounting of their experience.

Breaking down binaries is another place where compositionists are attempting to invoke Deweyian theories, but would benefit from more serious examination of Dewey's theories and Fred Newton Scott's use of them. For example, current compositionists often try to break down such binaries as student/teacher, masculine/feminine, and academic/personal discourse. Siegfried, a philosopher, points out that current pragmatist feminist thought, derived from Dewey and his followers, critiques dualisms as oppressive (113). Likewise, current compositionists see the difficulties inherent in binaries as oppressive and counterproductive and work to break them down. Much like philosophers, compositionists work with binaries such as the one between academic and personal discourse. What is valued as academic discourse in the classroom? If teachers allow students to write about personal experiences, even connected experiences, are they putting those students at risk of then not knowing how to write an *academic* argument? Likewise, in only allowing students to pursue academic argument, do teachers silence students and devalue the experiences Dewey found so valuable? Progressive Era scholars, however, did not see this in the way we do. Even asking the question about personal essay versus academic argument shows that we continue to create binaries even as we mean to dismantle them. Progressive Era teachers instead saw personal experience as a stepping stone to academic argument, encouraging students to make personal connections to material in order to make academic arguments about the material. They are steps on a continuum. Students cannot write any kind of paper without relying on their own personal experience, and its connection to other things they know and are learning. The work of Clara Stevens, who is discussed further in Chapter Three, makes it clear that the dichotomization we currently create between academic and personal writing would be, to her way of thinking, an incorrect interpretation of Deweyian connected experience. To place personal experience and academic experience in two separate categories would have resulted in a nonproductive student experience. Stevens, for example, notes that the whole purpose of the writing course is to help students "organize and express" their experiences ("College English" 109). Stevens believed in having students connect their experience to any discipline about which they were learning (110). For her, there was no clear reason for a division between academic and personal—they were interconnected and needed to be used with one another in order to give the student power in expression: "overcoming difficulties, giving at last clear and adequate expression to his experience, the student has a degree of mastery, of power. This power will be increased in a series of actions and reactions" (101). Stevens's words are clearly Deweyian and clearly feminist—she wants students to have power, and she wants them to get this power through connected experience. This constant, cyclical nature of gathering thoughts and ideas, relating them to what a person already knows, and working to express that in an organized way ultimately blends the personal and the academic so that a clear division is no longer visible. The personal becomes academic, the academic personal.

Feminism, composition, and Deweyian progressivism clearly intersect in multiple ways. As Walker, Geertsema, and Barnett summarize, feminist pedagogy "encourages participatory learning, personal experience, social understanding and activism, and critical thinking" (185). These are all key components to Deweyian pedagogy, and to current progressive composition pedagogies as well. Feminism has much to say and to connect with in Deweyian progressivism and it is clear that current compositionists would do well to reread progressive scholarship. However, the relationship still seems one-sided, and it is clear that modern scholars and teachers, especially in composition studies, would benefit from conversation that emphasizes the effects Deweyian progressivism can have on feminism and its applications to their field.

Limits to Deweyian Progressivism

While it may seem I am making Dewey into a champion for feminism, progressivism, and writing instruction, Dewey's work had its limitations, especially in terms of gender. Dewey has been heavily criticized for essentializing women, and indeed, his writings repeatedly reflect this. While he was surrounded by strong, educated women, he seems to have a limited vision for the roles women might occupy. Repeated examples in his works include women as nurturers—mothers and teachers in particular. While these were typical roles for Progressive Era women, Dewey does not seem to have thought of a role for women outside of education (especially at the lower levels) and family. He also contributed to the essentializing of women when he notes that "the continued participation of women in society will add a moral dimension to social situations" (Seigfried 100). Seigfried indicates that Dewey's attitude was similar to most of the pragmatist philosophers. According to her:

> It seems to me that Dewey successfully challenged some prejudices against women and supported women's rights, but he did not deepen his analysis of the causes of women's oppression nor extend these insights into his thinking in general because, like many other male philosophers, he neither shared in women's experiences nor was sufficiently motivated to focus on women's issues. (12)

Dewey's failure to focus on these issues leads to one other problem between Deweyian theory and composition. Deweyian theory is often seen as feminine, complete with its examples of the nurturing mother.

The maternal view of the teacher was actually directly reinforced by the progressive tradition, and Dewey's work is no exception. Redding Sugg, in *Motherteacher: The Feminization of American Education*, notes that Dewey's vision of creating a supportive atmosphere where no person (and especially no child) would feel intimidated caused a solidification of the role of the mother-teacher (183). Modern composition scholars such as Suzanne Clark, Susan Miller, and Eileen Schell have offered significant debates on the cost of this kind of caring, both for teacher and student. While this approach has allowed feminist teachers an outlet for exploration and has reinforced Deweyian pedagogy, such an approach has also retrenched the notion of composition as women's work. While there are certainly benefits to the use of this type of pedagogy (see Griffin, Middleton, and Schell), it continues to feminize the field of composition and therefore jeopardize its status as an intellectual and rigorous discipline within the university. Unfortunately, the use of Deweyian pedagogy in composition studies can further feminize composition.

Overall, Dewey also clearly underestimated the power of gender issues (as well as wholly ignoring issues of race) when he created his theories, but their use value to modern scholars overrides their sexist overtones. Regardless of his flaws, Dewey appeals so strongly to modern feminists, especially those in composition theory, because of his complex theories of transaction and development, his clear call for social change and questioning of social roles, and the continued direct application of his theories to the writing classroom.

In addition to Dewey's limitations with gender (and race), Deweyian theory also tends to emphasize working toward wholeness and synthesis (which Dewey views as achievable goals). This fails to take into account issues of power and difference, which are always present in social interactions (in particular, the classroom) and cannot always be resolved. For Dewey, interdependence on others is wholly achievable and desirable, and through the web of pragmatist connected experiences, differences should be minimized (Seigfried 99). In part, Dewey may not have given this area as much attention as current scholars because of the more homogenous nature of the student bodies he taught.

Conclusion

Deweyian progressivism never became the dominant educational model in the United States, and many of his views are unknown to current scholars, even as they invoke them. Nevertheless, despite Stanley Aronowitz and Henry A. Giroux's claim that "Dewey's best ideas are all but lost to American educational practice" (21), certain instructors did (and do) utilize them—knowingly or unknowingly—in the composition classroom. Aronowitz and Giroux's contention is correct overall in that the majority of the models Dewey espoused were lost to administrative progressivism. It is important, however, to recognize that Harvard's influence, while far reaching, was not all-encompassing, even within its own walls. While theories of teaching often look stable, they are complex and often do not address the often harshly pragmatic nature of classroom pedagogy. While history usually paints a bleak picture of theme-grading, grammar-grubbing, unhappy instructors merely biding their time teaching composition until they could teach literature, the reality is not quite so grim. Progressive Era scholars such as Sophie Chantal Hart, Clara Stevens, Fred Newton Scott, Gertrude Buck, Walter F. Barnes, Lane Cooper, Edwin Hopkins, June Rose Colby, and Elizabeth Hazelton Haight make it clear to modern readers that all was not lost in the wash of Harvardization. Pockets of progressivism continued long after Dewey, and modern composition has reclaimed and retained many of Dewey's best theories. Fred Newton Scott's Department of Rhetoric at the University of Michigan offered a place for such work. In addition, women's education in the late nineteenth and early twentieth century offered a site for the implementation of Deweyian progressive practices. The next chapter explores Dewey's influence on writing instruction, in particular through Fred Newton Scott and Scott's training of graduate students. Dewey's influence, as this evidence will show, was much more far-reaching than he himself most likely ever knew, and it is imperative for any critical imagining of progressive education to include discussions of Dewey.

2 Fred Newton Scott and the Legacy of Deweyian Progressive Writing Instruction

And, indeed, one of the characteristic features of Mr. Scott's work in theoretical as well as practical rhetoric, has been his sense—a sense which he has imparted to his classes—that writing is not a pyrotechnic exhibition of fine phrases, or an ornamental addition to the bare truth of things, but the direct, natural reporting of what one has one's self seen and thought.

—John Dewey

Lift up your hearts. We are not here to drill pupils in spelling, punctuation, and grammar, but to bestow upon them the potentiality of service to thousands and perhaps millions of their fellow countrymen—to develop in them the power to move humanity to noble deeds by the communication of the truth.

—Fred Newton Scott

As part of any critical imagining, Kirsch and Royster advocate for deep listening, derived from original sources (649). This listening involves understanding what those sources have to say and seeing them in relation to the historical, social, and political events of the time. In imagining what progressive pedagogy and its influences on writing instruction might have looked like, any scholarship is remiss if it leaves out a discussion of Fred Newton Scott, the founder and chair of the University of Michigan Department of Rhetoric from 1889 to 1926 and the ultimate American representative of Deweyian progressivism in writing instruction. Scott argued tirelessly for Deweyian progressive methods for teaching writing. Influenced by Dewey himself (and in fact a co-instructor with Dewey on occasion when Dewey was teaching at Michigan), Scott developed a theory of the teaching of composition-rhetoric that reinforced Deweyian progressive notions of teaching and learning, which he saw as imperative at both the secondary and collegiate levels. Susan Elizabeth Thomas, in her 2002 dissertation on Fred Newton Scott, writes that Scott's plan for education in rhetorical studies was progressive and organic in nature, and reflected Deweyian beliefs about secondary school and university collaborations. She notes that Scott "became more and more interested in interdisciplinary approaches to learning and incorporated Deweyian pragmatism into his attempts to unify the efforts of secondary schools and universities" (65). In addition to his progressive work to establish a relationship between secondary and university education and espouse progressive notions of writing instruction nationwide, Scott also helped train many other progressive scholars and teachers through his scholarship and the unique graduate program in rhetoric that he developed at the University of Michigan.

There is enough information available about Fred Newton Scott to render a substantial critical imagining of his life and work. Born in Terre Haute, Indiana, in 1860, Fred Newton Scott's higher education began at the University of Michigan, where he graduated with a Bachelor's degree with a concentration in languages in 1884. Scott was much influenced by the work of Dewey, who had served on his dissertation committee for his PhD (completed at Michigan in 1889), and it was indeed Dewey who recommended Scott for a position at Michigan (Stewart and Stewart 13). Donald C. Stewart and Patricia L. Stewart warn that over-emphasizing the influence of Dewey on Scott would be inappropriate, though, since "from what we know of Scott's education before he ever met Dewey, and the fact that he was but one year Dewey's junior, it might be safer to conclude that Scott and Dewey were philosophically compatible, that they found in each other intelligence and ideas which mutually reinforced each other" (14). Regardless of their relationship, their combined influence on the history of rhetoric and on writing instruction is considerable and often unrecognized.

Despite the fact that the work of Dewey and Scott did not ultimately become part of the dominant models of education, it is difficult to understand how someone like Scott achieved such prominence and recognition within his field but remains virtually unknown to modern readers.[1] However, Scott was very active and well-known during his lifetime. His visibility in national activities helped him gain both prominence and recognition relatively early in his career. He was the only person to ever serve two consecutive terms as the president of the National Council of Teachers of English (NCTE), in 1911 and 1913 (122). As well, he served as president of the Modern Language Association in 1907 (96). He published prolifically, and he attended conferences locally, nationally, and internationally. His very visibility to the rest of the world, combined with a conscious effort to meet and work with other people within his field, clearly contributed to his success. His combination of writing theoretical articles as well as textbooks made his name, if not his reputation, more visible as a greater number of composition-rhetoric instructors searched for texts that would help them teach writing, a pursuit most of them were wholly untrained for. Scott also did his best to maintain relationships with high schools, and frequently participated in the conference of the North Central Association of Colleges and Secondary Schools (75) as well as the Conference on Uniform Entrance Requirements (123).

Recovering Scott's work and theory and imagining what they might have looked like in the context of the Progressive Era, how they might have functioned for the women who later used them, and how they socially circulate with current theories of the teaching of rhetoric and composition is easier with Scott than with many. He was extremely prolific, and while his textbooks mostly reflect market forces and tend to be more conservative, his publications give a substantial view on his theories. Student reflections and memorial tributes also offer a window into Scott's world and in particular give insight into his teaching methods. In addition to reading published resources, I also examined three boxes of Scott's papers at the University of Michigan Bentley Historical Library. These contain a variety of types of correspondence, both with university officials and former students, daybooks with nearly daily journal-type entries, and other documents Scott saved throughout the years as important (including an invitation to join the Ford Peace Ship in 1914 and correspondence with a company for a patent for a new type of glasses he developed). Scott's papers and notes reveal a multifaceted person interested in writing, journalism, and linguistics. They also show a very human (and often humorous) side to Scott as he writes about adventures with his children, his attempts to learn how to drive, his love for animals, and the loss of his wife. Such a collection of records allows me to more fully rescue, recover, and reinscribe Scott's work in ways I could not otherwise. Unfortunately, I am still left to critically imagine large pieces of it. In particular, very little seems to have survived in the way of syllabi that might tell me more about how Scott organized his courses. However, the abundance of information I do have about Scott allows me to critically imagine his life and work more clearly than would be possible if these documents did not exist.

The combination of Scott's prolific work and his own notes provide multiple examples of Deweyian progressivism in writing instruction. He used aesthetics, psychology, and linguistics (all newly developing fields) in his Deweyian approach to writing and rhetorical theory. Throughout Scott's work, his focus on the individual as an active participant in the learning process, his denigration of continually encroaching standardization, his view that students were active members of a democratic society and active classroom participants, and his work to train others in his methods all become clear (Stewart and Stewart 18; Kitzhaber 223). James Berlin, in *Rhetoric and Reality*, describes Scott's rhetorical theory as "the most complete embodiment of John Dewey's notion of Progressive Education, reflecting his convictions that the aim of all education is to combine self-development, social harmony, and economic integration" (47). Berlin labels Scott's rhetoric as a "unique American development, a rhetoric for a modern democratic state" (47). Scott advocated for a voice for all people, and his was a communal and democratic theory rather than an individual one. As Thomas explains,

> given the astonishing theoretical similarities between Scott and Dewey's theories on teaching and educational reform, it seems the originality of Scott's work lies primarily in its adherence to Deweyian educational and social philosophies and its commitment to progressive reform. In other words, Scott, unlike most of his colleagues in the English Department, was attuned to educational and social concerns that transcended the university and sought to incorporate these concerns into his pedagogy. (2–3)

Scott's continued research, collaborations, and publications all reflect these ideals.

While Scott's theories and practices of writing instruction are replete with Deweyian theory, perhaps one of Scott's strongest Deweyian ideals was his respect for students as individual knowers. Evidence of Scott's focus on the individual is clear throughout his publications and papers, as well as student descriptions of his work. He clearly viewed students as active, knowing individuals, and he focused on their individual needs rather than offering them singular advice meant to cover all bases. Among his papers at the University of Michigan is a set of general directions for students that read much more like something from Peter Elbow than from the 1890s. In these directions, he encourages individuality in his writing students. He asks his writers to think about their own work habits, and to use them—writing at whatever time of day they write best, establishing a writing schedule, using an outline if it is helpful, but not being too wedded to it, keeping the audience in mind, and writing as simply and as clearly as possible in order to help the reader understand (Stewart and Stewart 25). In addition, Scott actually designed an assignment with the purpose of having students think closely and critically about their own habits and abilities as writers. Under the heading of "Methods of Work" are the following questions from the assignment:

1. Do you compose rapidly or slowly?
2. Is your first draft generally the best you can do, or are you in the habit of making numerous changes and corrections?
3. What is the most difficult part of the task of composition?
4. Under what conditions do you produce your best work, as for example, when you are at leisure or hard-pressed, when you are alone or with others who are writing?
5. Do you write better with or without an outline?
6. If you use an outline, at what state of the work do you prepare it? (Give your natural inclination and actual method of work, in case these differ from what you have been taught or from what you believe to be the right method of work.)
7. What form does the outline, if you use one, naturally assume when you are planning an essay?
    a. Do you see, in imagination, the heads and subheads in tabular form? or
    b. Do you hear the words or pronounce them to yourself? or
    c. Do you feel your ideas "move" in a certain direction?

8. Does an outline in tabular or bracketed form give you much idea of the contents of an essay or satisfy you in any way?
9. Do you, when writing, picture to yourself a hearer (or audience) or reader? If so, of what character, grade of intelligence, etc.? (Give details.)
10. Do whole sentences or paragraphs shape themselves in your mind before you write them? If so, what form do they take? Do you see them (visualize them) or hear them?
11. Do you read your sentences aloud in order to test the rhythm? or punctuation?
12. Are you apt to talk to yourself when composing?
13. Can you dictate readily? (qtd. in Stewart and Stewart 26)

Scott's focus on having students understand themselves as writers is clear. The examination of an individual's writing habits and composition process can lead the student to examine the self as an individual writer as well, with the ultimate goal of improving writing practices and ultimately the finished products. Through these questions, it is clear Scott understood the writing process in a different way from those who sought to teach grammar as a method for helping students learn to write better. The questions above present a far different focus—one of understanding writing as a complex technology, differing from individual to individual, instead of a set of discrete skills that could in any way be generalizable. Scott also clearly encouraged his students to imagine themselves as writers.

Seeing the writer in his or her social context was vital to Scott, and has been socially circulated in current theories, although it is doubtful most current users of such a theory have any clear idea of its origins. For example, Lester Faigley, in his 1985 article "Nonacademic Writing: The Social Perspective," faulted writing theory for separating the textual, the individual, and the social. Like Scott, Faigley found this dichotomy disruptive and divisive for writers. "Surprisingly, Faigley's sentiments were expressed almost verbatim some eighty-five years earlier by Scott and Dewey, particularly the emphasis upon the social and the social forces which shape an individual and the rejection of the disparity between public and private language/thought" (Thomas 151). Having writers understand their environment and the forces that have shaped them was as important for Scott as it is for modern composition instructors.

Scott makes his respect for students and their writing processes known throughout other scholarly publications as well. For example, in Scott's essay about writing at the University of Michigan, published in William Morton Payne's *English in American Universities*, Scott describes his own pedagogy as representative of writing instruction at Michigan. Helping individual students improve their ability to express their thoughts in a clear and connected manner is Scott's primary goal. In accomplishing such a goal, Scott describes his aims and methods as threefold: "first, continuity and regularity of written exercises; second, much writing, much criticism, and much consultation; third, adaptation of method to the needs of the individual student" (Payne 121). Notably, Scott felt that the third aim was the most important in ensuring the success of student writing, and noted that the ability of the instructor to "somehow lay hold of the student as an individual is, for successful composition work, simply indispensable" (121). Scott's use of the word *consultation* shows his belief that students should have input into their own writing process; his use of student conferences and the active practice of writing as a way to learn to write, as well as his individualized sense of the writer, are all clearly articulated in his words. This key focus on the individual, and the resulting development of a personalized form of writing instruction are reflected in the pedagogical and theoretical work of compositionists in the 1970s, particularly in what Berlin calls the transactional rhetorical movement. Thomas makes direct connections between Scott's theories and current theorists, noting that the works of Edward P.J. Corbett, Janet Emig, and Linda Flower and John Hayes are all reflective of Scott's personalized approach to writing instruction (145).

Descriptions of Scott's classes also reflect his pedagogy of inclusion and his respect for writing as a process. Rhetoric 23/24, a graduate course Scott taught at Michigan for many years called Seminary in Advanced Composition, was largely based on workshopping the writing of the students involved, with minimal lecturing. The 1908–1909 Course Catalog description reads, in part:

> This course is intended for a limited number of advanced students who write with facility and are in the habit of writing, but who desire personal criticism and direction. Although the greater part of the time will be spent in the discussion of the manuscripts submitted for correction, there will be talks upon

the essentials of English Composition and the principles of criticism and revision. (127)

Student texts were clearly the focus and assigned reading for the class, with limited lecturing from the instructor. In a 1980 interview with Donald C. Stewart, former Scott student Jean Paul Slusser recalled the seminary as a class where students "brought in whatever moved us to write or do in writing . . . so we wrote and wrote if we felt like it. If we didn't feel like it, we didn't. But, we didn't waste our time" (Personal Interview). Seminary was a place for students to receive feedback on their writing in a workshop environment that Scott facilitated. Slusser described Scott as "reserved," and noted that as a teacher, he pressed students to do their own work. "He kept his distance and just let you turn yourself inside you quietly through his subtle influence" (Stewart, Personal Interview). Scott's work as a writing teacher, then, clearly involved a much more sophisticated approach than lecture and grammatical correction. In addition, Scott's own statements reflect a pedagogical belief in the teacher as facilitator in both the writing process of individual writers and in classroom discussion. In the preface to a 1917 printing of George Henry Lewes's *Principles of Success in Literature*, Scott offers advice to teachers using the text, and in doing so promotes his own seminary teaching methods. Scott advises instructors:

> This book may be used in the classroom in a great variety of ways. The writer's preference is for what may be called a rudimentary form of the seminary method. The members of the class are not asked to recite as from a text-book, but, having read the treatise, or a portion of it, with much care, are encouraged to discuss with the instructor and with one another, as many of the important points as time will allow. Advantage may be taken of the interest thus aroused to suggest other lines of reading. In this way the student will be led to undertake original research, and ultimately, perhaps, to do a little independent thinking for himself. (3–4)

Such a method reflects a pedagogy of inclusion that is progressive, discussion based, and student focused. In addition, it demonstrates a pedagogy that asks students to engage with the material rather than rote memorization. Student development was personal and personalized. Essentially, Scott was developing early writing workshops for his students.

The idea of students as active participants in the writing classroom and their own writing process is also clearly articulated in *Aphorisms for Teachers of English Composition* (co-written with Joseph Villiers Denney) when Scott gives lengthy advice to the teacher for approaching student writing:

> The main question which the corrector of themes should put to himself is not, How many errors can I find in this theme, but, How can I help the writer to improve? The whole class should be enlisted in this effort as they listen to the teacher's rapid reading of impromptu themes immediately after the writing. Let the class participate in the correction; let them commend; let them disapprove; but let them always understand that the sole object is to help the unknown writer to a better expression of the idea which he would communicate. When teacher and class are in this attitude, reproof is robbed of its sting, and criticism is eagerly sought. (14)

Scott's teaching style and general pedagogical beliefs become clear here. Workshopping papers in the classroom was obviously valued, and students were expected to provide feedback for their peers as well as work on their own texts. As Thomas notes, "instead of rules, Scott taught discovery. Instead of superficial correctness, he advocated meaningfulness, anticipation of consequences, and audience awareness" (23). Using this method, the teacher is a facilitator rather than a corrector, a guide rather than a director. Scott very much believed, like Dewey, that students needed to be involved in their own instruction. In Scott's pedagogy, constructive feedback and attention to the individual writer are both valued. Stewart seconds this observation in "Rediscovering Fred Newton Scott" when he notes, "Generally speaking, Scott says that good theme correction should be individual, constructive, rational, systematic, and informed by common sense" (544). In addition, the classroom was a place for students to be actively involved in the writing process. Remarkably, *every* student, whether they were in a graduate seminar or a freshman rhetoric class, was expected to be a participant. Shirley Smith, a former student but also the Vice President and Secretary of the University of Michigan, recalled in a memorial tribute Scott's successful work in getting students interested in and appreciative of the power of language. According to Smith,

> It was astonishing until we got used to these discussions how heated even a football guard or a prospective chemist who had elected the course wrathfully because it was required work, could get over such questions as whether an ice-coated branch glittered or glistened or glowed in the winter sunshine, or what noun would best convey the successions of sounds of blows exchanged by mailed knights in mortal sword combat. (280)

Such exercises emphasized the importance of language and offered students ownership of their own work. According to Smith, it was ownership in which they were able to take pride. In addition to his publications, Scott's preference for seminars and his inclusion of students in working projects (he collaborated successfully with a number of his students, including Gertrude Buck) further demonstrate his pedagogy of inclusion.

Having students involved in their own learning also relieved the tedium many other instructors faced with a purely lecture/recitation model. In that model, instructors' experiences must have varied little, lecturing on the same information and grading themes constantly. Having students workshop the themes would have resulted in better writing, which would have meant less correction. As well, Scott didn't "correct" the themes but engaged with them dialectically, which meant he was not simply working as a constant proofreader but engaging with ideas. Student participation would also have kept conversations in the classroom fresh, as different groups of students focused on different aspects of the writing process. Scott's daybook includes an ironic entry about his first interaction with George P. Baker, of Harvard fame. It also offers an insightful comment about the difference in their teaching styles. Scott writes: "Conference at Teachers College. Baker a short mild man with reddish brown moustache. Asked me if I really meant what I said about enjoying the reading of essays" (Diaries and Daybooks, February 22, 1905). While Scott suggests that he did enjoy working with student essays, his daybook also suggests, as I have above, that student discussion and classroom participation kept his own thinking alive and vital. On November 12, 1903, he wrote:

> Lively discussion in class in appreciation over question whether anything was gained by study of technique of verse. Spoke with a little warmth and found myself afterwards a little ex-

> cited but at the same time morose with little batteries of arguments sputtering in my mind like fire-crackers. Worked in the afternoon a little on outlines, but could not get question of technique vs. intention out of my mind and spent some time setting down haphazard suggestions.

Clearly the class discussion spurred Scott's own thinking and writing and kept his interests in the field from stagnating.

In addition to valuing the individual, Scott had different priorities for the writing process than many of his contemporaries. According to Scott, a good idea is more valuable than a grammatically clean essay. Scott notes that good ideas are much easier to develop into good essays, but grammatically correct essays many not contain any good ideas. Good ideas can be more clearly articulated, especially through careful and constructive revision, whereas well articulated papers without substance are much harder to improve (Scott and Denney, *Aphorisms* 13). Revision of a good idea can also offer clear insight into a student's growth. Clearly then, part of Scott's approach included constructive critical feedback, addressing issues of style, voice, tone, and elements outside of the purview of grammar.

In addition to valuing students as knowers and viewing writing and the teaching of writing as complex and process-oriented, perhaps one of the most Deweyian aspects of Scott's pedagogy was his assumption that knowledge must be connected in order for students to make sense of it. As a result, Scott felt that asking students to write on topics that were unfamiliar to them or not interesting to them would result, naturally, in poor essays. In his textbook, co-authored with Denney, Scott and Denney offered the lists of topics that had become so prolific in textbooks of the time period. Scott and Denney, however, suggested topics that were "in sharp contrast with the similar lists found in earlier texts," instead offering topics to which students might either be able to relate or might find out about with limited investigation (Kitzhaber 107). Scott repeats the advice to create assignments based on familiar topics (or ones that might be interesting and exciting to learn about) in *The Teaching of English in the Elementary and Secondary School* (1903), co-written with George Rice Carpenter and Franklin Thomas Baker. As Stewart notes, in *The Teaching of English* Scott cautions teachers that they will have to read the papers they assign, and "suggests that student interest in subjects may be stimulated by connecting the subjects to be written about with those already known to be interesting to students; by piquing their curiosity on new subjects; by giving them practice in converting abstractions into concrete language, and by providing constant enthusiasm and support" (544). This attitude is also reflected in Scott and Denney's *Aphorisms for Teachers of English Composition*, when they advise, "Never say to them, 'I want you to be interested in this subject.' Interest them" (10). Scott's emphasis on this is critical to his pedagogy. Students who are not interested in the topics they write about will not, as modern compositionists have often observed, write to the best of their ability.

Scott also believed students should be trained to carefully observe the world around them and sought to interest them in looking for details. He created what he called artifact assignments, where students would observe a painting or a statue in order to write an observation of what they saw. Student Emily Wolcott described one such assignment in a letter home. On March 9, 1903, she told her mother, "we had all written essays explaining the expression on the face of a bust of Emerson, by somebody Morse. The two sides of the face are very unlike, and the front is different still—It was hard enough to write. The bust has been standing in the Eng. reading-room table for several days, and has been scrutinized and twisted and turned by the hour." In addition to training students in observation, this exercise also created community and allowed for collaborative brainstorming and pre-writing among the students, who would gather around each piece of art and discuss their observations before beginning their essays. It also created a topic that was common to the entire class, but was at an individual student's disposal to *know*. While they were not necessarily experts in art, they had the common experience of being observers, of looking carefully at an object to test their powers of observation.

As well as believing a student could not write well about a topic to which they were not connected, Scott also believed students could not make sense of grammar and rules of usage without the connected context of their own writing. It is worth reproducing a lengthy section of the Memorial written about Scott by his former students at Michigan in order to better understand his overall philosophy of grammar and its place in the writing process:

> Of course, he was not concerned more than the conventions required with the mere chores of spelling, punctuation, and dictionary righteousness which most of us had once and with good reason considered the over-mastering purpose of com-

position teachers. But he looked on words as a cabinet maker looks on his tools—things that just must be right and unabused throughout or the work will be bad. The tools were not what he was making: it was the product that basically interested him. His concern was with living ideals and emotions and how they might be formulated and how they might be transferred from mind to mind or soul to soul with the least of power. In so far as we responded to his treatment we came to look on the misuse of a word much as an artistic woodworker would look on employment of a chisel for screwdriver purposes; it was childishly destructive of a necessary tool. (Smith, S. 279)

Importantly, though, Scott did not feel that if the student as carpenter used the tools of the trade incorrectly the entire house would fall. Rather, he recognized that student error was a part of the text, and that correcting it involved using the underpinning text itself to do so ("What the West Wants in Preparatory English" 19). Scott repeats this view in *The Teaching of English in the Elementary and Secondary School* when he notes that a teacher should "cease to regard [grammar] as a study merely of abstract rules and formulas; he should come to see that the underlying subject is virtually the same as that which underlies composition and literature, namely, the expressive and communicative activities of the English speaking race" (in Stewart, "Rediscovering" 544). Again, Scott's view reflects a complex understanding of grammar as a part of the writing process. Grammar, to Scott, was integral to, not separate from, other parts of the composing process.

Scott, like Dewey, also did not believe in standardized testing. Nor did he believe in the entrance exams Harvard (and many other colleges, especially on the east coast) had begun to demand of entering students. Scott felt such standards forced teachers to teach with the test in mind, rather than focusing on the individual learner. He was in agreement with Dewey on this principle, as Thomas notes. "Dewey supported, along with Scott, a university admissions policy based upon student diplomas from accredited institutions rather than upon satisfactory marks on an entrance test. Dewey, like Scott, recognized the futility of 'teaching or studying to the test,' as it violated the principles of meaningful learning, discovery, and growth" (Thomas 73). In an article titled "What the West Wants in Preparatory English," published in *The School Review* in 1909, Scott questioned standardized testing practices and their results: "If, instead of keeping his eyes upon his students' progress and estimating their worth by the growth of their personalities, the teacher is compelled to keep one eye on his class and the other on a set of examination questions, what will be the natural consequence? Is he not likely to acquire a squint?" (12). Scott also felt this was an east-west issue, since so many eastern colleges and universities (and so few western ones) required entrance exams. He describes the results of such a burden on teachers, specifically ones in the east:

> But no one can deny, I think, that certain eastern teachers are much more preoccupied with the problem of getting particular boys into particular universities than are any western teachers. It is my observation that the burden of preparation weighs heavily upon them. And why should it not when failure to get a candidate through the university gate is accounted as little less than a crime? It would be strange, indeed, if this continual pressure did not sooner or later make crooked the teacher's standard of judgment. ("What the West Wants" 12)

Many of Scott's arguments are repeated in modern debates about standardization and teaching to the test. Scott, like Dewey, was fighting a battle against administrative progressivism in an effort to avoid what he saw as the inevitable result of standardization: lack of commitment to individualized instruction; standardized needs over personal (and intellectual) ones; and a defiance "of accepted principles of education and the suggestions of common sense" (14).

Scott also eschewed the results of standardization in "Efficiency for Efficiency's Sake," which was originally given as a speech to the North Central Association of Colleges and Secondary Schools in 1914 and later published in a collection of Scott's works. Speaking against the ways in which the efficiency movement had picked up on the use of standardization, Scott noted that such an approach fails to record or measure things that are not quantitative, but are still of vital importance in measuring student growth. "They are things such as personality, sympathy, sincerity, enthusiasm, intuition of character, taste, judgment, love of truth, tact. These things are qualities, not quantities, and any judgment of them, to be adequate, must be made in terms of quality" (52). Many writing instructors still struggle with ways to measure such characteristics today, and to quantify attributes that should instead be qualified. Scott, like Dewey, believed writing well should be a life-long process, not one that can simply be mastered at the lower levels and then abandoned. Harvard, for example, wanted to make writing instruction the sole purview of the secondary schools, and eliminate the courses at the college level. Scott, in contrast, wanted to make composition instruction more effective instead of getting rid of it. From Thomas's point of view, "while Harvard was thinking of university interests and the reputation of its faculty, Scott was, as ever, thinking of his students and what would best serve them" (20). Despite his influence in educational arenas at all levels, Scott's desire to see fewer standardized methods of teaching was all but ignored, and standardized testing and rote memorization (both considered more scientifically measurable than the individual work of Scott's methods) continued to remain dominant in all levels of writing instruction across the country.

Scott also worked tirelessly in order to combat the notion that composition was drudge work, and that the teaching of writing should be used as a stepping stone toward a position in literature. Scott *had* to work tirelessly in order to continuously combat the Harvard reports and the pervasiveness of academic progressivism. Like Dewey, Scott believed progressive education in writing could help students achieve their own influence in a democratic system. Scott continually worked to undo the constructions schools such as Harvard continually worked to uphold: that college was somehow a separate part of the educational system from elementary and secondary education; that college was solely the territory of the elite; and that writing instruction should be reserved for those in need of remediation (Stewart and Stewart 22). In contrast, Scott saw the goal of composition as primarily a practical one. In his 1895 description of the University of Michigan's undergraduate program in rhetoric, he commented that

> the aim is not to inspire our students to produce pure literature, if there be any such thing, or even help them to acquire a beautiful style. If we can get them first to think straight-forwardly about subjects in which they are genuinely interested, and then, after such fashion as nature has fitted them for, to express themselves clearly and connectedly, we will have done about all we can hope to do. (Qtd. in Brereton 179)

Scott's goal was certainly an admirable one, and it offered composition a reputable place within the university that unfortunately never established dominance.

While Scott's theories and pedagogy were fundamentally important to him, overall his greatest success and greatest remaining legacy was the formation of his Department of Rhetoric at the University of Michigan. Scott began his tenure at Michigan in 1889, upon the completion of his PhD. By 1903, he had developed such a strong program and attracted so many students that he was able to successfully petition the university for the creation of a new department. The Department of Rhetoric was chaired by Scott, and all indications point to a peaceful and relatively nondisruptive separation from the English department. Stewart and Stewart, in *The Life and Legacy of Fred Newton Scott*, observe that the department of English had long undergone name changes, and that Scott's control over the majority of the rhetoric courses anyway made the separation a fairly natural one (53). As chair, Scott developed three types of courses: the first intended to give practice in narration, description, exposition, and argument; the second to introduce the "fundamental principles of rhetoric and criticism;" and the third a combination of advanced composition work and critical theory (Stewart and Stewart 55). These core courses continued in various formats throughout the life of the department. In addition to a concentration of composition courses, Scott also developed courses in journalism and graduate studies in rhetoric that were among the first in this country. In fact, for many years Scott's program was the only program that offered graduate degrees in rhetoric in the United States. It also numbered among a handful of graduate programs in the late nineteenth and early twentieth centuries that offered graduate degrees to women.[2] One good measure of the success of Scott's graduate program is its rate of graduation: despite its status as a new department, between 1904 and 1930 the Department of Rhetoric granted 140 master's degrees and twenty-three doctorates. Comparatively, the University of Michigan Department of English granted twenty-four doctorates (Berlin, *Rhetoric and Reality* 55).[3]

Scott's teaching methods, as described previously, were Deweyian progressive in nature, and this had a tremendous effect on his students. At both the undergraduate and graduate levels, he was described as using a Socratic question-and-answer discovery method of teaching, and encouraged students to learn material critically instead of through rote memorization. Wilfred Shaw's description of graduate studies in rhetoric in *The University of Michigan: An Encyclopedic Survey* gives evidence of the Deweyian progressive influence in the department:

> Graduate study in rhetoric was characterized throughout the existence of the department not only by a broadly liberal point of view in linguistics, with a consistent emphasis upon the growth of language as a social phenomenon and as an instrument for current needs, but also by critical attitudes which had their bases in psychological investigation and in an examination of literature in its relation to life. Merely historical matters were subordinated to the analysis of works and to an understanding of the principles by which their authors wrote and of the sources and modes of their appeal. Scott's own deep humanism permeated the work of the entire department, and graduate study in rhetoric became synonymous with an earnest search for central standards in artistic creation and aesthetic response. (562)

Shirley Smith, Vice President and Secretary to the University of Michigan, seconded this description in a memorial tribute to Scott and commented directly on Scott's teaching approach. According to Smith it would have been easy for Scott to simply *tell* students what he wanted them to learn from the day's lesson. Instead, though, he "probed, searched, cross-examined, students all round the class, spending the time trying to get and generally getting before the bell rang, the criticism or comment he felt was justified or needed" (279). While it was a much more difficult approach for the students who had to do the work of arriving at Scott's point, Smith notes that they learned much more this way (as with any critical approach to teaching) than if they had simply been handed the information. Scott's interests in psychology, linguistics, and aesthetics, as well as his Deweyian approach, clearly impacted his classroom practice.

While all of the above material contributes to my knowledge of Scott, my critical imagining of Scott as a professor is further fed by descriptions of his teaching facilities. Scott taught for many years in the Rhetoric Department offices in West Hall. The building was repeatedly condemned by the administration and finally razed in 1924 (Shaw 565). The circulating joke on campus was that the way to tell freshmen to find West Hall was to have them push against each structure—the building that shook was West Hall (Stewart, Personal Interview). Thousands of old student themes filled the basement (and much to my researcher's sense of horror, were left there when the building was pushed in). Scott and the Rhetoric Department began their residence of West Hall in 1903 and so the most robust years of the rhetoric program were spent there. Shaw describes the building as already ancient and in need of demolition when the university acquired it. "It had no private offices and sometimes as many as four instructors would be holding conferences in the same room at the same time. It was so crowded that a passageway less than ten feet wide was used as a classroom, and another of the same sort as office and library" (565). Shaw wryly comments that for some students the building represented a "nightmare of required themes," but for the rhetoric students in particular

> it was a place of light and inspiration. For here were situated the rhetoric library . . . and the seminary room of Professor Scott. Scott's room was unique. It contained more than a thousand books, among them his valuable private collection in rhetoric and criticism. The walls were plastered with pictures, some of them copies of masterpieces, some of an unusual, grotesque sort. Many were prints from foreign magazines, *Jugend*, for example; and there were photographs of gargoyles and caricatures of great literary figures. Completing the scene were the round table, around which the seminary students sat, and Scott himself, remembered by many as a sort of fixture in the room, comfortably ensconced between the table and his desk, which was always piled high with papers, lecture notes, and books. (565)

Students recalled the seminary room fondly in memories gathered from a variety of sources. Helen Ogden Mahin, in "Half-Lights," the tribute that she wrote for Scott as one of his former students, remembered "there was talk of everything conceivable that had to do with beauty and truth, art and humanity. And to at least one student the dust, the books, the pictures, and the voice of the preceptor were like the song of the wind in the branches, sweeping over all the things of the earth" (2). When asked to include an "outstanding memory" on the University of Michigan's 1924 Alumnae Survey, former student Ruth Mary Weeks also fondly recalled the seminary room, noting that her favorite memory was "Professor Scott conducting a round table in his roomy old office." It must have been a large room, indeed. When former department member Thomas Rankin went to teach at Carleton College, he requested a similar space in his 1931–1932 annual report, nothing that "at the University of Michigan we had for departmental reading alone, for the department of Rhetoric, a reading room seating 300 students" (6). It is possible, then to imagine Scott in a large room, with his messy desk, gathering his seminary students around him to discuss writing. It is a romantic picture, especially as Mahin portrays it, but one that helps to complete my imagination of Scott in his environs.

Scott's Far-Reaching Influence

In part because of Scott's professional levels of activity, and in part because of his reputation, the Department of Rhetoric attracted women and men from across the country to undertake graduate work. Some came for the intensive writing workshops and later became fiction writers. Others, however, were more focused on progressive pedagogy and would train in this area with the goal of teaching writing at the college level.

It is impossible to name all of the graduates from the program and their successes, and indeed, the next two chapters are devoted solely to two of them. But naming some of them provides a larger picture of what they did and the influence they in turn were able to generate. Through such a list, it is possible to see the vast social circulation of Scott's ideas. Lawrence Conrad, for example, worked under Scott and later became a teacher and author at the New Jersey State Teachers College at Montclair. Of creative writing, Conrad wrote, "the setting for a class in creative writing should provide an atmosphere in which the student can believe that his own thoughts and his own experiences and his own feelings are intensely real and are as important as anything he might read out of a book" (in Adams, *A Group of Their Own* 48). Such words might have been written by Scott himself. The fact that Conrad taught at a teacher training college was also significant in that it meant he was training teachers who would then influence their own students in turn.

Ruth Mary Weeks, another example, is rarely discussed by modern compositionists, perhaps because of her focus on linguistics. Kitzhaber, however, describes Weeks as a leader in "the movement that tried to promote a more liberal and scientific view toward language matters in composition courses and textbooks" (73). Using similar language, Stewart and Stewart describe Weeks as a leader "in the movement to establish descriptive linguistics" (40). Weeks later became a president of the National Council of Teachers of English, and continued to publish her research in journals such as *English Journal* (Stewart and Stewart 4, 153).

Sterling Andrus Leonard, a faculty member at the University of Wisconsin, was another of Scott's students who continued his work. Leonard focused, like Scott, on students' rights to their own language. As Berlin notes, Leonard waged a "campaign against the insistence on distorting the student's language and life to conform to the biases of a narrow class interest" (*Rhetoric and Reality* 51). Leonard also published two books regarding the social basis of rhetorical discourse: *The Doctrine of Correctness in English Usage, 1700–1800* (1929) and *Current English Usage* (1932) (*Rhetoric and Reality* 88). Leonard, like Weeks, was also president of NCTE (Stewart and Stewart 4).

Future professor Ada Snell also worked directly under Scott for her graduate work. Snell would go on to be a professor at Mount Holyoke College, and in 1942 would write a history of the English Department that is a key source of information for this book. Snell's work with Scott focused primarily on poetry and cadence rhythms, a topic of great interest to Scott, who published several papers on it. Scott later served as editor for Snell's book, *Pause*, published in 1918 by Scott's series, *Contribution to Rhetorical Theory* (Stewart and Stewart 44).

One of the most notable and famous of Scott's students in rhetoric and composition was Gertrude Buck, who went on to do extensive work in composition and rhetoric at Vassar. Buck shared many of Scott's beliefs regarding pedagogy, and also published extensively.[4] Buck's dissertation, published by Inland Press in 1899, was titled *The Metaphor: A Study in the Psychology of Rhetoric*. Even the title reflects the Progressive Era concern with psychology and linguistics in rhetorical study. Buck notably also recommended her own undergraduates pursue work at the University of Michigan. Correspondence between Buck and Scott reveals the influence she was able to exert.

Particularly amongst Scott's female graduate students who went on to teach, the influence of Scott becomes clear. When Kirsch and Royster discuss the idea of social circulation, they note that it "invokes connections among past, present, and future in the sense that the overlapping social circles in which women travel, live, and work are carried on or modified from one generation to the next" (660). Such social circulation is particularly evident among Scott's graduates who taught at women's colleges. These initial students of Scott created what Margaret Rossiter calls *protégé chains* when they left the University of Michigan but continued Scott's work in their own classrooms. They ultimately created a vast network of progressive writing instructors across the country. In turn, for as long as they could, they recommended the University of Michigan graduate program to their own students. After their students pursued their graduate work, women's colleges in particular would often hire them back, bringing Scott's influence full circle (Eisenmann 41).

Perhaps Louis Strauss, a member of the University of Michigan's English department, articulated Scott's influence on his students best. Strauss comments that "under the spell of his magnetic and stimulating personality his students developed to their utmost capacity. They are to be found everywhere—brilliant teachers, successful writers, and men [and women] in every walk of life upon whose tastes and characters his influence is indelibly stamped; and they are not backward in saying so" (332). This is echoed in Shirley Smith's memorial tribute to Scott, in which he comments "there must be hundreds of teachers of English in this country who though they never saw Scott knew perfectly well that their practical success has been made possible through methods invented by him" (280). While Strauss is referring to Scott's influence on his own students, Smith's comment indicates the extent of Scott's influence above and beyond his own students. While Scott is often thought of primarily as a teacher, his scholarship and his professional activity reached a great many more people than his teaching alone.

FRED NEWTON SCOTT, DEWEYIAN PROGRESSIVISM AND THE SEVEN SISTERS

In critically imagining Scott's life and work and listening deeply to it, part of it came back to me with a resounding echo—I could see his life and work resonating loudly in many of the modern theories in rhetoric and composition I knew. Kirsch and Royster require that good feminist scholarship in the history of rhetoric and composition ask questions, such as "what more lingers in what we know about [the people we study] that would suggest we think again, to think more deeply, to think more broadly?" (648–49). In Scott's case, thinking broadly and deeply allows us to see that his work was in no way isolated, and in fact impacted many others in the field. Scott's influence reached far beyond the students who studied under him or read his work. In fact, a lineage for the influence of Scott's work can be established through his students. Students of Scott's left his classrooms and used his models of Deweyian progressivism as they began their own collegiate teaching careers. In many ways, Scott's theories and his use of Deweyian progressivism traveled well beyond Scott, as his graduates and followers adapted his methods for their own use. One particular place Deweyian progressivism proliferated was in the English departments at eastern women's colleges.

Some background about women's education at this time is necessary in order to see the influence of Scott and Dewey in particular locations. While the very notion of educating women at this time was seen as progressive, women's enrollment continued to climb during this period, and by 1920 women comprised 47.3% of the college population (Newcomber 46). The development of schools that educated women in the United States was seen as a progressive and feminist project on a very basic level. If one of the main shared goals between feminism and progressivism is social change, especially through education, then the very project of providing educational opportunities for girls and women fulfilled that goal from the outset. This is not to say that the Progressive Movement writ large necessarily defined all women's colleges and girls' schools as progressive. Nor did all progressive thinkers believe women should be educated. Rather, the Progressive Movement continued to contribute to the shape of an already existing project. During this time, the Seven Sisters colleges developed their academic programs and participated in progressive curriculums and activities.

The Seven Sisters colleges were devoted to the education of young women.[5] By the turn-of-the-century all seven of the schools offered advanced curricula for women that were comparable to men's colleges. As they developed, they "abandoned preparatory departments, attracted a better-educated and more distinguished faculty, set up student self-government associations and honor codes, founded campus branches of settlements and other reform organizations, broadened their perspective on women's careers, and competed with each other in athletics and debate" (Gordon 8). Women students were also involved in Progressive Era social reform, including suffrage, temperance, teaching, social work, educational reform, labor reform, public health nursing, and home economics.

English studies was no exception as a site for progressive activity. The English departments at Smith College, Wellesley College, Mount Holyoke College, and Vassar College in particular manifested strong progressive programs. Catalogs reflect English programs that were actually similar to the graduate program at Michigan; Mount Holyoke, as noted earlier, even had an undergraduate major in rhetoric, as well as a course in the teaching of rhetoric (Berlin, *Rhetoric and Reality* 56). Despite what some research conjectures, female students at the Seven Sisters participated in all aspects of English studies, including rhetoric, composition, oratory, debate, grammar, and elocution. Course catalogs show this clearly at the four schools listed above. Many of the programs used Dewey's notions of integrating students in organic relationships with their environments and encouraging them to write about topics they were both familiar with and interested in. As Miriam Brody points out in *Manly Writing: Gender, Rhetoric, and the Rise of Composition*, students with Deweyian progressive instructors were imagined in organic relationships to their environments, and "because the writing process was arduous, the writer was encouraged to think before writing, representing a landscape of thought outside language. Organic notions of writing supplied new representations of an old idea, an essential writer and [her] writing were interconnected [sic]" (163). Writing was seen as connected to the writer, and ideas were seen as stemming from the writer's experience.

Deweyian notions of teacher-student relationships to writing were also invoked. For example, Vassar's 1876–1877 catalog offers evidence that the theme exercises, so often vilified in composition history, were also offered at Vassar. Under the leadership of Gertrude Buck, the effect of Deweyian progressive pedagogy was clear, and theme exercises were designed to be interactive and dialectic activities between instructors and students. Whereas at other places devoid of Deweyian influence, themes were often corrected by instructors who might not even be attached to the course, Vassar's approach was quite different. The College Catalog states that evaluation of themes was "minute, personal, and free, being made in personal interviews between the teacher and the students individually." Buck's influence on this aspect of the program is clearly Deweyian.

By the early twentieth century, writing instruction and the women's colleges listed above had both been highly affected by the developments and social changes of the Progressive Era. In 1917, Elizabeth Hazelton Haight, Vassar professor, offered a telling description of pedagogy at Vassar when she notes that professors are "eager to make the young think for themselves, to get their personal reactions to the material placed before them, to make the class-room a civic institution of community effort, where each person shall perform his civic duty of thought" (16). Such attributes, according to Haight, had been adopted by female instructors as well as males, at women's colleges as well as men's. The Deweyian overtone of democratic education is clear in Haight's description, and Haight's prescription for classroom teaching presumably carried over into the writing classroom in many institutions. Student reflections on the teachers at these institutions also reflect progressive practices: Socratic dialogue, multiple paper drafts, and close student-teacher relationships are described in student reflections and memorial tributes.

Fred Newton Scott and the University of Michigan graduate program were both clear influences on many of the women teaching at these colleges. Proof of Michigan's influence exists in even more tangible ways than the progressive pedagogies previously described. Women graduates from the University of Michigan's rhetoric program were heavily represented in the English departments of Mount Holyoke, Vassar, Smith, and Wellesley. This becomes clear in a 1919 transcript of the Intercollege Conference on English, which was held at Mount Holyoke College and involved representatives from the four colleges. Of the nineteen women present at the conference, six had graduate degrees from the University of Michigan, including three PhDs (Mastrangelo 415).[6] Another participant would receive her PhD from Michigan in 1924, and one participant who held a master's degree (Sarah Hincks) would receive her PhD from Michigan in 1922. Clearly this common connection had an impact on their conversations, which centered around such topics as entrance exams, placement of students into writing sections based on writing samples, and grading procedures, all topics of concern to Scott (and some to Dewey). Their shared training gave these women a shared educational background and shared experience from which to talk about important departmental and co-curricular issues.

These women also followed Scott's example of longevity. Scott spent over forty years (1884–1926) working on various aspects of rhetoric at the University of Michigan. Likewise, many of the students he mentored were long-standing faculty leaders on their campuses. Clara Stevens, for example, spent twenty-seven years as the chair of the Rhetoric department at Mount Holyoke College, and Sophie Chantal Hart worked in the Rhetoric department at Wellesley for forty-five years, spending many of those as chair. Scott's longevity was in part the reason for his tremendous influence, and this was true of his students as well. Longevity allows for the creation of long-serving institutional connections, insights, and power structures. In large part, these men and women created powerful personas on their campuses that were largely reflective of Scott's. Like Scott, they were able to create and maintain departments that were largely associated with them as individuals.

Many alumni of the University of Michigan's rhetoric department also gave Scott direct credit for his influence. Clara Stevens, who is discussed extensively in the next chapter, cites Scott and Dewey as direct influences on her thinking. In responding to a 1924 Alumnae Survey, she answers the question of how she would characterize the influence of the University on her life by supplying the following: "As I was at the University of Michigan only one year and a term (the first term of 1891–2 and the year 1893–4) I did not really know the University. But to the three men with whom I worked, Professor Scott, Professor Dewey, Professor Demmon I owe much of intellectual stimulus." Her teaching reflects the influence of these men, and in particular, the Socratic method of Scott, which I discuss more extensively in the next chapter.

Mary Yost, who was a member of the English department faculty at Vassar for a number of years, graduated with her PhD from the University of Michigan in 1917. Yost made a comment similar to Stevens's in her response to the survey, noting that "the stimulus to independent thinking and to gaining an organic philosophy was given me richly by Professor Scott [. . .]." Gertrude Buck also acknowledged Dewey and Scott directly in the Introduction to her dissertation: "To Dr. Scott I am indebted for much stimulus and criticism in the preparation of this thesis; to Dr. John Dewey, now of the University of Chicago, for the fundamental philosophical conceptions embodied in it" (iii).

Like many others, Buck also exerted influence on later students, influencing their graduate school choices and recommending they go to the University of Michigan. In 1913, for example, Buck wrote a lengthy informal recommendation, recommending Sarah Hincks, Vassar class of 1910, to Michigan's graduate program:

> My dear Professor Scott,
>
> Miss Sarah Hincks, Vassar, 1910, tells me that she has written to you applying for an assistantship in English. She writes me that you gave her to understand that the list of applicants is already very long and I suppose that means that there is slight probability of her receiving the appointment. She would, however, I believe, be an excellent assistant. Her quite extraordinary good looks have tended to discount her ability, I think, but this is very genuine. She is the daughter of an Andover theological professor and has a peculiarly honest and finely penetrative mind. Her poetry is the best writing that she does and that has a singularly exquisite quality, though its range is limited. She has proved an admirably successful teacher in Miss Wheeler's school in Providence, (I think that is its location) and her practical and administrative efficiency has been as completely demonstrated there as her more purely intellectual and aesthetic gifts were during her college course. Miss Wylie has often spoken of her as a future member of our own department so you may know we think as highly as possible of her. (Scott, Personal Correspondence)

There is no extant response, and so it is impossible to know if Buck's letter had an impact on Hincks's admission to the graduate school, but the dates do correspond—Hincks was admitted for graduate study for the 1913–1914 year, completing her AM and graduating in 1914. It seems quite likely Hincks might also have known Mary Yost, who would have been doing earlier course work during the time period Hincks was in residence. This is more likely given a letter that exists from Buck to Scott, in which she inquires after the progress of both Hincks and Yost. Dated October 11, 1913, Buck writes: "I hope Miss Yost and Miss Hincks will do us credit in your work" (Scott, Personal Correspondence). Clearly Scott must have replied to her, because another letter, dated October 18, 1893, has Buck writing to Scott: "I am delighted that Miss Yost and Miss Hincks have made so favorable an impression upon you and upon others. I think further acquaintance will wholly justify it" (Scott, Personal Correspondence). Rossiter's protégé chain was completed when Hincks was offered a job at Mount Holyoke. In April of 1917, then department chair Clara Stevens wrote to Scott, saying "I want to thank you for your note about Miss Hincks. Your word and that of Professor Wylie added to Miss Snell's comments make us confident that we want Miss Hincks" (Stevens, Personal Papers). Hincks, however, decided to return to her alma mater and is listed in the 1919 faculty of Vassar College.

Further archival evidence also supports both Gertrude Buck's influence in trying to convince students to go to Michigan, and the influence of the Michigan program on its graduates and their students. In 1912, Helen Drusilla Lockwood, a senior Vassar English major, wrote the following in a letter home about her graduate school decisions:

> I have given up Michigan for I think we have gone crazy for it here for several of our English instructors are from there. And Professor Scott is quoted on all occasions so that I really feel that I wouldn't be getting such a very new point of view if I were studying with him for Miss Buck and Miss Wylie are both devotees of his work, methods and ideas so I guess I would rather go to Columbia.

Lockwood did indeed complete a PhD at Columbia in Comparative Literature. While Lockwood was not directly influenced by Scott, her letter reveals that Scott's progressive pedagogy had a lineage; teachers were leaving his program and influencing their students with pedagogy that was directly influenced by him.

Women faculty who were Deweyian progressives had two advantages as they pursued their work. In part, their work at women's colleges was often overlooked and unchallenged. They were therefore able to create and maintain progressive programs for their students, with little outside scrutiny from administrative bodies or even parents. In addition, the women who graduated from Fred Newton Scott's program were extremely well trained to teach composition. Their work at the University of Michigan and the community it later afforded them are testimony to Scott's influence.

Other faculty at Michigan were also aware of Scott's influence, particularly on women from the Seven Sisters. Louis Strauss, a professor of English Literature who had observed Scott initially create the rhetoric department, realized Scott's national standing and ability to attract students. Strauss recalled that "the new department flourished and grew amazingly. Graduate students flocked from far and wide to work with this brilliant scholar; the women's colleges in the East, in particular, sent their most promising aspirants to academic careers for practical and scientific training under his guidance" (331). Scott's reputation for the finest training in rhetoric was not only well known among his students and graduates, then, but also among other members of the university community.

Scott's influence in other arenas, however, was not as strong. Scott's life work was spent in an attempt to battle administrative progressivism in writing instruction. Unfortunately, his career paralleled Dewey's in many ways, including the fact that his never became the dominant model for writing instruction. Kitzhaber notes that "he tried, though unsuccessfully, to secure the adoption of a fuller conception of rhetoric, one that would restore to it the great social importance that it has sometimes had in its long history. Unfortunately, English teachers were not ready then to accept such a view" (73). The Department of Rhetoric, which was described as coming into being mostly at Scott's insistence and under his will, was also impossible to extricate from its leader. Stewart and Stewart note that he himself had developed most of the courses in the department, and continued to teach them (53). When Scott began to move toward retirement in 1926, taking several semesters of leave in a row, the University began an attempt to abolish the department. Richard K. Harmston's research reveals that Scott had long been criticized for not securing adequate pay for instructors in the department, and had worked under several university presidents who saw the work in rhetoric as unimportant (13). Thomas, too, finds that Scott's lack of strong administrative ability and inability to respond to change were key elements in the department's downfall. According to Thomas, Scott's "colleagues in the Department of Rhetoric claimed that Scott lacked the administrative skills to support his vision for the department, as he neglected the professional development concerns of his staff, resented constructive criticism and even rejected suggestions for improvement" (5).

In addition to the lack of leadership and vision on Scott's part, Stewart and Stewart emphasize the importance of the Hopwood Awards in the Rhetoric Department's demise. Avery Hopwood had donated a large sum to the Department of Rhetoric to be used for a creative writing award. The English Department was apparently anxious to control the award. In the *Michigan Alumnus Quarterly*, Roy Cowden (who later administered the award) recalled the remarks of Professor O.J. Campbell as he announced the award: "he introduced his remarks by saying that in joining forces with the Rhetoric Department the English Department was apparently marrying an heiress" (in Stewart and Stewart 205). In addition to such political and financial maneuvers, as later chapters also show, the 1930s was an especially volatile period for universities financially, and consolidation of departments and administrative services at this time would have been desirable and practical. As well, most other major midwestern universities had a united department of English. Due to failing health (and badly failing hearing), Scott retired from the department in 1927. In 1930, the Department of Rhetoric and the Department of English were merged into a single department. Dean Effinger, the dean of the university, noted that in terms of the Department of Rhetoric, "Scott had been the 'personal inspiration [which] was responsible for its peculiar success,' and with his retirement, there was no longer need for the separate entity" (in Stewart and Stewart 203). Any remaining connection with the department ended with Scott's death in 1931.

While it seems that such a short-lived program would have had little overall influence in the larger sense, Scott's influence over his thirty-year career was indeed far-reaching. Even after his retirement, Scott continued to profoundly influence many of his students throughout his life and theirs. The next two chapters discuss two of Scott's graduates who ran the English programs at Mount Holyoke College and Wellesley College respectively, and the ways Scott influenced their work.

3 Clara Stevens and the Mount Holyoke College English Department

> *The higher education of women is a feministic movement, the natural expression of a fundamental principle that is that women being first of all human beings, even before they are feminine, have a share in the inalienable right of human beings to self-development.*
>
> —Mary Woolley

> *She was one of the really great teachers, and her influence and inspiration has been one of the most treasured gifts of all my life. That she could bring such powerful stimulus to people, when she was so frail in body, and so utterly gentle in all her dealings will always be to me one of the miracles of the spirit. But it is a beautiful experience to have had and I cherish it.*
>
> —Mary Ashby Cheek, John Martyn Warbeke, and Helen Griffith

A critical imagining of the teaching of Progressive Era writing can involve many different paths, including imagining the teaching of female students at women's colleges. This area has been a key place for recovery work and much of this work has been "grounded in and points back to the pioneering women, both contemporary and historical, who have insisted on being heard, being valued, and being understood as rhetorical agents" (Kirsch and Royster 643). In seeing the Progressive Era as a feminist movement, recovering and imagining the work of female teachers with female students is a key component, one that allows me to "think again about what women's patterns of action seem to suggest about rhetoric, writing, leadership, activism, and rhetorical expertise" (650). Through such a lens, it becomes clear that while the Progressive Era offered multiple opportunities for young women to go to college, it also offered the opportunity for the first generation of college professors to teach. College-educated women, while still not encouraged to teach at many of the large research institutions, were both needed and welcomed at many women's colleges, particularly the Seven Sisters. As departmentalization occurred in the late nineteenth century, many chose to teach English in some form. Many progressive English teachers, often trained under Deweyian influence at places like the University of Michigan, entered women's colleges and began to make changes to extant programs.

It is difficult to recover pedagogy from any time period, since records of actual instruction and the day-to-day work inside of individual classrooms is rarely recorded. However, archival material, including student notebooks, department meeting minutes, faculty papers, and memorial tributes, can offer glimpses into the world of female composition pedagogues during the Progressive Era. According to Rynbrandt, "archival research is especially useful for the process of recovering potentially important, yet little known individuals, institutions, and social movements in the past, whose stories may not be readily available in more traditional documentary sources" (13). As I have previously stated, in doing research on Mount Holyoke College's rhetoric program, I was fortunate to find documentation regarding the work of one pedagogue in particular. As I was working to track down the origins of the rhetoric program, one of the Mount Holyoke archivists brought Clara Frances Stevens to my attention. In reading Stevens's papers, I was surprised to see exactly how progressive her teaching seemed to be. Familiar at the time only with the history of Harvard's nineteenth-century writing instruction, I had no idea such progressive pedagogues even existed.

In critically imagining the history of the teaching of English studies at Mount Holyoke, I relied heavily on archival documents. English department papers from Mount Holyoke's archives are quite extensive and include department memos, secretaries' notebooks, teaching notes, student journals, student notes, and letters. Occasional syllabi, exams, and student papers also exist. One department document I rely on substantially to supplement my critical imagining is an unpublished manuscript by Ada Snell, a Mount Holyoke graduate from the class of 1892 who later became an English professor at the college. Snell was herself a graduate of the University of Michigan program and was an active Deweyian progressive teacher and scholar, as noted in Chapter 2. Snell was approached by the college in the mid 1930s and asked to write a history of the department of English and of English studies as a whole. Her information was to be included in a 1937 centennial publication about the college. Snell did not complete the manuscript until 1942, and as a result, it remains unpublished. However, her research project was similar to this one. In compiling her history of the department, Snell made extensive use of many of the department's existing papers, her personal knowledge of the college and its programs, and her proximity to early faculty members make her history of the department particularly valuable and well-informed. As a result, Snell has left a comprehensive and important historical document of the department's activities and structure up until that point.

The Mount Holyoke archives also houses the faculty papers of Clara Frances Stevens, the English department professor who created and maintained the department of Rhetoric (later English) from 1884 until 1921. Stevens was a key figure in the development of the department and in the Deweyian progressive changes the department underwent throughout her tenure. Stevens's papers include department memos (written by Stevens), notes, personal letters, and memorial tributes. As well, I have explored the only three academic articles Stevens ever published professionally. The first, published in 1906, is titled "College English" and was published in *English Education*. The second, from 1907, is titled "A Suggestive Report," and was published in the *Journal of Pedagogy*. A leaflet, "The Ethics of English Work" (1903), was published by the New England Association of Teachers of English. The existence of these papers, along with other English department papers, has made this critical imagining possible.

Like most institutions, Mount Holyoke's history of writing instruction went through various phases. Early writing instruction at the college was administered by Mary Lyon, the school's founder, whose progressive notions of education were implemented throughout the curriculum. Beginning in the 1850s, however, following Lyon's death, the school altered its pedagogy in order to follow the more current-traditional models of its brother schools. This was done in an attempt to remain current with the hegemonic models and texts in use at the time. Later, in the 1880s, Clara Frances Stevens, herself a Mount Holyoke graduate, helped return writing instruction at Mount Holyoke to its former progressive state. After Stevens's departure in the 1920s, however, and coincidental with the arrival of a particularly conservative new president, writing instruction again lost its progressive focus. Tyack and Cuban, in *Tinkering Towards Utopia*, note that these cycles of change are typical of educational systems in the United States. Such ebbs and tides are the results of shifting sociopolitical conditions and directly affect the administration of any social programs, including education (53). Mount Holyoke was no exception. Understanding their curriculum not only strengthens my critical imagining and strategic contemplation of it but also helps me in "developing interpretive or sense-making frameworks" (Kirsch and Royster 663) about my information.

Early English Studies in Mary Lyon's Seminary

Before any critical imagining of Clara Stevens and her program is possible, it is necessary to understand the history of Mount Holyoke College and its early writing and rhetoric program. Even early on, English was an important subject at Mount Holyoke. Mary Lyon, the founder and first leader of Mount Holyoke, was said to have valued the ability to write as being "perhaps the highest qualification for usefulness" (Snell, "History" 1). Lyon was also familiar with Hugh Blair's works, and it remains probable that she agreed with his statement that writing was the means by which "men secure influence over one another" (in Snell, "History" 6). Because writing at the beginning of the nineteenth century was closely linked to class structure, literate people were those of the upper class, those who literally wrote the rules, both social and legal. Lyon in fact had more of an understanding of English studies than was most likely the case for many other institutional founders at the time; she had taught English at Zilpah Grant's Ipswich Seminary. Her views are reflected in her correspondence, particularly with Grant. In a letter to Grant in 1832, she wrote: "I wish some way could be contrived to have the English language studied with as much intensity as the Latin is. I have a few floating ideas upon this subject" (Hartley 36).[1] Lyon based her own methods on those she had learned from Grant. Both women espoused methods of learning that were similar to those of Pestalozzi and Friedrich Froebel, focusing on the child rather than the teacher. In her own words, Lyon believed "a teacher should be careful not to appeal to herself. Let your actions speak. Make the dull ones think once a day; make their eyes sparkle once a day. Let your punishments be such as affect the mind, not the body" (Hartley 390). Her attention to the student as an individual is clear. Sarah D. Stow, in her 1887 *History of Mount Holyoke Seminary During its First Half Century* also noted Lyon's beliefs (similar to Pestalozzi's) in life-long learning and process over product. "Taught to place mental power above acquisition, they learned to regard learning as an unending process, not a finished attainment, and to consider its continuation a duty" (105). While Lyon's methods were infused with Protestant doctrine, her beliefs in the knowledge and power of her own pupils took precedence. She clearly supported the various facets of rhetorical education, designing early courses in grammar, logic, and rhetoric. For these courses, Lyon chose Lindley Murray's *An English Grammar* and Richard Whately's *Elements of Rhetoric* as required texts for the first class of students at Mount Holyoke. Murray was a text she had used at Ipswich (Hartley 61, 144).

Rhetorical education was implemented at Mount Holyoke when it first opened. Whether for future influence, individual education, or teacher training, Snell noted that "rhetoric, under whatever name, has always been taught at Mount Holyoke. It remained as a department heading even when the subject itself had expanded into several courses, and it was not dropped until 1897 when the word English was substituted" (5). From the college's founding in 1837 until 1855, however, the term *rhetoric* was used to describe "English studies, exclusive of composition. [Rhetoric] in these years was simply the name of a single course" (5n). Composition as a course was taught separately, and although it is not always clear from the historical record where the delineation between the two subjects was drawn, it is probable that the rhetoric course focused more on studying grammatical and stylistic matters, as well as matters pertaining to forms of persuasion, whereas the composition course probably focused more on the actual practice of writing. Early courses in rhetoric utilized the popular texts of Blair, Samuel P. Newman, and Whately, and later courses list Hill and John Franklin Genung as the primary texts.[2]

Early in the college's curriculum, written records show that Lyon also required rhetoric as a study for juniors and seniors. Rhetoric was, in fact, a required course for both classes until 1844, and Snell notes that Lyon chose her texts based on what she found other, older colleges using as well as texts she had been exposed to at Ipswich (2). She relied mostly on course texts borrowed from other institutions, including Amherst, Harvard, and Yale, in order to design courses that included study in grammar, elocution or reading, rhetoric, and composition. These texts remained, with very few changes, for the first twenty years the college was open.

Information about the texts in use can help supplement a critical imagining of the overall rhetoric program. Originally, the junior text was Newman's *A Practical System of Rhetoric*. Blair's *Lectures in Rhetoric and Belles Lettres* and Whately's *Elements of Rhetoric* were among the required texts for seniors. While it was not listed in the course catalog among the texts for the class, Blair was listed among the texts on which seniors were examined (Snell 5). Whately is listed in course catalogs until 1858. Whately's belief that students must have interesting topics for compositions appealed to Lyon, who encouraged students to write about diverse topics that were of interest to them.

It is difficult to know where Mount Holyoke stood in relation to most other schools in terms of its entrance requirements and textbook use, as many schools did not have course catalogs (or particularly extensive course catalogs) in the early nineteenth century; as a result much of the information that would be helpful in making comparisons was not recorded. Harvard did keep excellent records, however, and can provide a point for comparison. Harvard's choice of textbooks is similar, and in some cases identical to those Lyon chose. Snell notes that, in planning courses in English, Lyon "merely appropriated what she found in the older colleges in the United States" (2). Nan Johnson's research for *Nineteenth-Century Rhetoric in North America* also lists Blair, Campbell, and Whately among the key nineteenth-century rhetoric treatises adopted as textbooks for both 1850–1875 and 1875–1900 (Appendix A, 251–53). Lyon clearly used texts she had encountered in her earlier teaching experiences, as well as those in other colleges she looked to as models.

The existing evidence shows that Mary Lyon designed the courses in rhetoric in a way that was generally reflective of the all-male schools Mount Holyoke was modeled after. Overall, Lyon's efforts to keep the textbooks cutting edge can be seen as those of a woman who was in touch with the rest of the scholarly establishment. Instead of Lyon's institution being an educational backwater, as is often the image of nineteenth-century women's colleges, Mount Holyoke was instead attempting to keep abreast of new developments. The uniqueness of the program lies in the fact that Lyon took these new developments to her instructors, who implemented their own pedagogies. While her overall model (and extant English department syllabi) resembled Mount Holyoke's brother schools, Lyon's student-centered focus was clear, and was quite unusual for the time. While her textbook choices may have been the same, pedagogically, then, she was doing something very different from her models. Snell notes, "she seems to have had ideas about writing that were independent of those held in her day" (13). That she allowed more liberties to her students from the very beginning than many schools allowed women after they became coeducational is shown in the structure of an English curriculum that included composition and debate, lectures and discussion as well as the opportunity for students to meet in Lyon's office and to talk through compositions with the college's founder. Snell offers a window into this practice when she recalls an incident from Caroline Goodrich Tyler (1851), when she was working on an English composition. According to Tyler, she met Mary Lyon on the street in South Hadley. When Lyon commented on her sad countenance and asked her what was wrong, Tyler said: "'I must write a composition.' 'O well,' she said, 'that's easy enough. I haven't much to do now, come to my room and I'll help you.' I gladly went. She asked what I had been doing lately. 'Have you had some good times?' I told her of an excursion. 'That's your composition. Write it just as you have told it'" (Snell, Part I, n3). It was through Lyon's careful guidance with subjects like writing that her students came to know her teaching. Her close involvement with students and her sense that subjects for written assignments could be derived from everyday experiences are also clear.

In the second half of the century, as the textbook usage indicates, the English program at Mount Holyoke continued to utilize its brother schools as models for their curriculum, especially Harvard. Mount Holyoke's later program became less progressive and more concerned with issues of correctness. A shift from the earlier, more student and content-based focus to a more current-traditional mode is clear in the second half of the nineteenth century. Mary Lyon relinquished her command of the college when she died in 1849. Snell noted that "rhetoric in Mary Lyon's time, as has been indicated, was a study rich in humanistic learning; this it gradually lost, and it was already in 1890 largely occupied with problems of usage" (25). Those who followed Mary Lyon, perhaps either because of a lack of progressive training or in an attempt to follow in her footsteps in looking to other colleges as models, were swayed by the pursuit for correctness at the expense of content. The change in rhetoric textbooks after 1858 marks a profound change in the pedagogy of writing instruction at Mount Holyoke. Such a change was also instituted at Harvard. In following a Harvard prototype more closely than ever, Mount Holyoke's rhetoric program at this time was progressive solely in that, instead of educating men to become scholars, it did so for women. What prompted the change is not particularly clear, but it was most likely due to outside influences, as well as a new presidency. Lyon's death left the school in the charge of several powerful women until a new principal could be appointed. Mary W. Chapin, an 1843 graduate, accepted the responsibility and was formally hired in 1851. Since other schools at that time were beginning to move away from a belletristic approach and toward a more formalistic program, it is likely Chapin also chose to move in that direction as well in order to remain competitive. In doing so, she selected George Payn Quackenbos's *Advanced Course of Composition and Rhetoric* and John S. Hart's *A Manual of Composition and Rhetoric* for the main composition texts. While both retained elements of belletrism, they were also highly prescriptive texts.

In the 1850s, the majority of schools required a course in the various forms of writing as part of their English studies curriculum, and Mount Holyoke appears no different in this respect. Most likely using other schools as a model for this as well, Mount Holyoke required instruction in the theme essays so popular at the time. Such themes, however, "were not meant to explore the inner self or to be regarded as truly expressive pieces of writing; rather they were to represent an individual perspective on experience, and so topics were never assigned" (Brereton 15). This was true at Mount Holyoke as well. In 1853, Sarah Dowd wrote to her brother: "We do not have the privilege of selecting our own subjects now, or rather we can select our own subjects but they must be of a particular kind, one week narration, another a description, and another some other kind" (Snell 14).

New textbooks were also among the changes course catalogs indicate. As stated above, both Quackenbos and Hart were required (Snell 14). Both were early inventive modes textbooks, and stressed style and the parts and pieces of the essay rather than writing as a whole. Such changes in the books reflect the move toward texts that focused less on ideas of invention or composing and notions of genius in composition and more on ideas of organization and different forms and ideas for writing.

Snell also makes clear that even in 1942, when she wrote the history of the department, she was aware of the class distinctions early writing instruction had begun to emphasize. In the mid to late 1800s, writing instruction, she correctly points out, had come to be the work of preparatory schools. Snell notes that instruction in English had been reduced to "the poor scullery maid scrubbing up the neglected English of entering students in order to make life easier for the academic aristocrats. The shift in the Seventies from rhetorical content, humanistic in nature, to one of practical techniques, tended to reduce composition work to a mere tool subject" (26–27). Correctness in writing was emphasized through practice, and content seems to have been of little concern. One Mount Holyoke student indicated in her diary as early as 1855, in fact, the emphasis on correctness that the program had come to entail, even twenty years before Harvard's declaration, and three years before the changes in textbooks were made at Mount Holyoke: "Poor Nell Tingley is feeling sadly because she had got to go into the spelling class on account of three mispelt words in her composition. She cannot leave it until she has written one hundred lines without a mistake either from carelessness or ignorance"[3] (Snell 15). As was typical at the time, course catalogs do not indicate a remedial spelling class. While one wonders how the distinction between carelessness and ignorance was made, this example nevertheless indicates something that is also not present in the course catalog—a preoccupation with correctness that matched or even superseded content. The study of style and of rhetorical expression was slowly abandoned during this period and replaced by a preoccupation with correct, if uninteresting and unimaginative, prose. The movement toward such correctness was partly an effort to maintain an upper-class status quo, separating out the educated elite from those labeled remedial, but the effects on the rest of the institutions in the United States and the history of rhetoric in general were profound.

Ultimately, while Mount Holyoke did pass through a phase in which they were primarily interested in correctness, this began to change again toward the end of the century. Other influences began to work at dismantling such current-traditional teaching methods as had been practiced at Harvard. By the 1890s, texts for rhetoric/English courses at Mount Holyoke included works by Dewey and titles such as June Etta Downey's *Creative Imagination* and H. A. Overstreet's *Influencing Human Behavior* (Snell 32). The result of such works was to refocus on the ideas of the student—in essence, to readmit the student as an active contributor to the writing process. Snell notes that such works as the ones listed above caused a shift from "what seemed a mechanical method to one which it was hoped would serve more adequately to cultivate worth-while experience and to express it in a natural yet orderly way" (32–33). In this way, order and standard could be maintained while also involving the student as part of the process. The shift in rhetorical education Snell documents was the direct result of the efforts of a new faculty member, Clara Frances Stevens.

CLARA STEVENS

As mentioned earlier, by the late 1800s, the English program at Mount Holyoke was a largely current-traditional one. One woman in particular was responsible for changing this. Critically imagining such changes requires investigating the work of Clara Frances Stevens. Because of the work of Stevens, or "Miss Stevens" as she was better known, the English department came to be a department devoted to a new and progressive brand of rhetorical studies. Stevens was responsible for the formation of English as a department and the reintroduction of the student as a knowing figure at Mount Holyoke during this time.

Stevens herself, like many of the other early faculty at the college, was an alumna. Born in Newburyport, Massachusetts in 1855, Stevens did not attend school until she was eight years old. She graduated from the Newburyport High School when she was seventeen, and although she wanted to start college immediately, economic circumstances prevented her (Cheek, Warbeke, and Griffith 222). After four years of teaching high school locally, she entered Mount Holyoke in 1878. She graduated from the school in 1881 and became a full-time member of its faculty in 1884, although she had been teaching Latin there since her graduation. She completed a PhM (Masters of Philosophy) at the University of Michigan in 1894, with a focus on courses in Rhetoric, Philosophy, Literature, and Aesthetics (Stevens, Personal Papers). Part of Stevens's later open-minded approach to education was a result of the influence of the study she undertook in philosophy in a department heavily influenced by progressive theorist and educator John Dewey himself. Stevens was fortunate enough to study with Dewey during his last few years at the University of Michigan, and with Fred Newton Scott as he developed his new program in rhetoric. Stevens studied in the program Scott was developing at Michigan, and was influenced by the approach to rhetoric as training for future participation in a democracy and the use of rhetoric as social and public discourse. Like Scott, she cited Plato as a key influence ("Clara Frances Stevens, PhM" 16). Stevens was also acquainted with Scott's most famous female graduate, Gertrude Buck, as evidenced by the fact that she and Buck coordinated a debate for students of Vassar, Mount Holyoke, Smith, and Wellesley. In addition, she and Buck were both present for at least one of the English conferences held at Mount Holyoke in the early 1900s (Mastrangelo and L'Eplattenier 122). Along with Buck, Stevens was also one of the first women to join NCTE after its founding in 1911 (Davidson and Wagner-Martin 212).

After officially becoming Mount Holyoke faculty in 1884, Stevens taught a number of courses, including Rhetoric, Latin and Modern History, Mathematics and Ancient History, and Mathematics and Rhetoric (Snell 27). Departmental formation occurred in 1897, and after that she taught solely within the department of English, which was separate from the department of English Literature. She remained in the department until her retirement in 1921, serving as its chair during the later years of her tenure. In an interesting note on an alumnae survey, Stevens observes that she became a professor in the department in 1904, even though she had been with the department far longer than that; "the title [of professor] not used in [the] college earlier" (Alumnae Survey of 1927). It is not difficult to imagine Professor Clara Stevens in her environs at Mount Holyoke College. Her house, which she shared with her sister Alice, still stands across the street from the campus. Many of the buildings in the center of campus were completed during the 1890s and early 1900s, and Stevens would have taught in them. Safford Hall dormitory, where Stevens was in charge from 1897–1904, still stands in the center of campus.

During her tenure at Mount Holyoke, however, the campus underwent tremendous changes. As the century progressed, more and more students were attending college. Departmentalization had been necessary in the 1890s in order to cope with the increase in numbers, even at smaller schools. Structural changes were needed as a result, even for Mount Holyoke. "Previous to this period, as for all colleges, each subject had been a single course; now each subject unfolded into many courses clustered in departments administered by highly specialized instructors" (Snell 26). As a result, courses like rhetoric, which had previously been a single course required of all students and was often paired with other, seemingly unrelated courses like mathematics, mutated into independent courses in both writing and speech. Student requirements also were revised; required hours in English were increased in 1888 from two to six, with English Literature demanding ten additional hours (Cheek, Warbeke, and Griffiths 223). Mount Holyoke's requirements were in keeping with other schools at the time. In Hermione Dealey's 1919 publication "Educational Research and Statistics: College Curricula and Interests of Women," Mount Holyoke lists fifteen combined required hours of English and English Literature. While this is far above the six required hours at Randolph-Macon College, it is in keeping with the sixteen hours required at Women's College, Delaware and the twelve required at Boston University's Women's College (294). In addition, Dealey found that English was elected more often at Mount Holyoke, Wheaton College, Randolph-Macon, and Goucher than any other course (294). Mount Holyoke students, then, both took a substantial amount of required English, but also elected to take English courses when they had room in their schedules.

The courses within the Mount Holyoke English department, however, grew to be unique. New courses were designed and overseen by Stevens. What is unique about Miss Stevens is her devotion and constant attention to the department of English as it continued to grow and change with the times. The college had been granted its charter in 1888 and became Mount Holyoke College instead of Mount Holyoke Female Seminary. Enrollment began to climb, and departments began to expand.[4] While there is no doubt others like "poor Nell Tingley" were still conditioned in unofficial spelling classes, Clara Stevens worked to return the picture of rhetoric to one that again included a much broader sphere. Part of this is no doubt due to Stevens's own commitment to a humanistic form of rhetoric and overall Dewyian influence, and part of this is due to the massive changes in the American college system and the effects of progressivism at the time. As the college continued to grow, so too did the department, expanding from just Stevens to include seven other female instructors by 1921, the year of her retirement. Stevens is also noted as having been the first person to design an undergraduate major in rhetoric, with electives ranging from persuasive writing to debates on contemporary issues (Berlin, *Rhetoric and Reality* 56). Expansion of the department also included more writing courses. In 1896, Stevens introduced both a course in Journalism and one in Playwriting.[5] Around 1897, Prose Style (also known as Theories of Style and Philosophy of Style) and History of the English Language were introduced. In 1897, nine courses were offered in English, of which Stevens taught six (Snell 28). In 1899, Stevens developed and taught Structure of the Novel and Drama. By 1901 Versification was also offered. Writing courses also included one in 1906 titled "Argumentative Writing and Debates," which was listed as a division of the larger course "Advanced Writing" (Cheek, Warbeke, and Griffiths 223). Writing out the debates beforehand was common practice, and the debate class at Mount Holyoke went through several incarnations, eventually becoming a club.[6]

The pedagogy behind the composition and rhetoric courses at Mount Holyoke, under Stevens's watchful eye, more closely resembled the original courses that had been offered at the college. During her thirty-seven year tenure, Stevens was able to make a number of changes to the ways rhetoric had previously been taught. Because Stevens joined the faculty of Mount Holyoke College at the very beginning of departmentalization, she was able to use her progressive training from Michigan under Dewey and Scott to create an influential and powerful department. This is indeed a unique opportunity for any instructor. She brought with her a humanizing and student-centered influence, much closer to Mary Lyon's original vision. Snell in fact credits Stevens with the move away from the current-traditional thinking of the day: "That Mount Holyoke revived the study in its richer aspects was owing to Miss Clara F. Stevens, whose quiet yet brilliant teaching, whose character and ideas carried weight with the Faculty to the extent that she was free to find her own teachers and to develop her field as, in consultation with others, she found to be most fruitful" (27–28).

It is difficult to discuss Steven's pedagogy from a modern perspective. It is anachronistic to use modern terms to describe what she was doing and when she was doing it, and it is difficult to resist putting words into her mouth. She never published an explicit statement of her pedagogy, and few students ever wrote about their experiences in her classroom. From what does exist, however, it is clear Stevens did participate in many of the manifestations of expressivist pedagogy that became associated with progressivism.[7] While her work was student-centered in that she believed that students had contributions to make to the classroom, and that students' questions and writing should be valued and respected, she did not in any way abandon direct methods of instruction. She ran a formatted classroom, taught structured classes, and met the specific demands of the department's requirements for majors. She believed college study should involve critical thinking and help students gain power. This becomes evident in her discussion of literature and writing in her 1906 publication entitled "College English":

> The college study of English literature and the college courses in writing should go far toward making our college graduates men and women of abounding and at the same time controlled life, and men and women of power. To this end literature must be studied as life and as art, and writing must have back of it and with it thinking so vigorous, and conviction and feeling so strong, that the student will steadfastly and courageously grapple with the problems of expression for the sake of voicing and reinforcing his thought and feeling. (101)

Stevens's belief that literature and writing instruction should not and could not be mutually exclusive of one another echoes many recent arguments in composition. In a department where most, if not all, writing instructors had backgrounds in literature it is easy to see where such a belief in utilizing literary texts as supplemental would not only be dominant but exclusive. Ironically, however, programs like Harvard's did not allow students to use any literary texts in the writing classroom, preferring instead to have students only write from personal experience (Brereton 11). It is possible to see differences, although sometimes subtle, between Stevens's program and others of the time.

In the above passage, Stevens's commitment to student expression is obvious, as is her passion that students should be allowed to express themselves, and their own views. Less expressivist views of education would not allow for such inclusion of *feeling*, while more expressivist views would ask that students be able to locate those convictions on their own. Stevens, however, felt that students' training in writing should offer them the ability to begin an almost scientific investigation "which collects data, weighs evidence, tries theories, draws conclusions, and presents them convincingly and persuasively; or any bit of interpretation which has back of it reading, assimilation, selection, organization, has its animating and controlling idea born of the writer's soul and mind [. . .]" ("College English" 104). Writing, for the students of Miss Stevens, like the students of Mary Lyon before them, was also a means to power and a lesson on how to lead the "controlled life." While this control did include extensive instruction in grammar, Stevens repeatedly stated in her 1907 publication that grammar instruction and drill was not to be seen as an end unto itself but rather "a means to correct, clear, effective expression of whatever one has to say or write on any subject to any person on any occasion" ("A Suggestive Report" 253). In a Deweyian progressive view very similar to Scott's, Stevens notes that grammar instruction and drill had to be oriented or contextualized in order for students to make meaning of it, thus making her a clear part of the Deweyian progressivist method of teaching grammar as embedded rather than acontextual (253). She also saw correct expression as a necessary tool for everyday life. When every student was able to "express clearly and truthfully what they see, hear, think, and feel, and effectively to communicate their ideas, colleges will have more able students and the world will have men and women more efficient because better equipped" (254). Student expression for Stevens, then, was a valuable skill that could not be overlooked.

From the recollections of her students, it is also possible to gain glimpses of Stevens's classroom practices and to critically imagine her at work. After her death in 1934, her pedagogy was described by former student Frances Warner Hersey, Class of 1911, in the *Alumnae Quarterly*:

> There was witch-work afloat of the most uncanny and inspirational variety; and yet, before the end of each hour, in spite of much spontaneous discussion, the definite work for the day had been rigorously covered, not a particle of our preparation wasted, and our minds made ready in an orderly fashion for what was to come next. Nobody was ever allowed to flap around in aimless circles, to be sure; but neither was anyone ever shot down in mid-air on the way to a destination, because of clumsy flight. (Cheek, Warbeke and Griffith 224)

It is obvious that Stevens allowed for discussion in her classroom, in contrast to the pure lecture format many of the traditional all-male schools continued to pursue. Stevens herself notes this in "College English," when she discusses the use of the lecture format as too often leading students to do nothing but take notes. She advocates a variety of methods in the classroom, including combining lecture, discussion, and writing, student lectures/recitations where students led the class, and "brisk and lively questioning" using the Socratic method (106–107). Hersey's recollection reinforces this; overall, Stevens's written theories of pedagogy were carried out in her actual practice.

A memorial tribute written by Marian MacGowan Evans, Class of 1904, also reinforces my imagining of Stevens as a critical pedagogue who valued student interaction. Much like the descriptions of Scott's students arguing about specific words, Evans remembered Stevens's course in descriptive writing as touching

> the ideal of education. We were not so much her pupils as fellow-seekers of The Highest. Together she and we were played upon, vibrated in response to the glory of words rightly used, the wonder of thoughts made incarnate through sound, to the miracle of black marks on a white page able to hold and to transfer the heart of genius, to catch and to pass on the majesty of life.

This exploratory approach to teaching words and language allowed students to find their own way with words and to navigate written language collaboratively. Student participation, as with Stevens's use of Socratic questioning, was a key to her pedagogy. It is an approach advocated for in modern pedagogy as well. As early as 1974, Donald Murray, in "Teaching Writing as a Process Not a Product" advocated teaching a process of discovery and exploration. Mirroring Evans's observations, according to Murray, "we work with language in action. We share with students the continual excitement of choosing one word instead of another, of searching for the one true word" (4).

It is also clear Stevens valued student voice, and encouraged individuals to speak in the classroom and express themselves in Deweyian progressive ways. For Stevens's students, this may have been the first time many of them had experienced semi-public forums where they were allowed to speak. Most importantly, she allowed those students' voices to both speak and to work through ideas in a supportive and protective environment, where students could explore and discover language.

It is rewarding to have such a description of Stevens's actual classroom. However, they are few and far between. Only one other seems to exist that offers the same kind of glimpse into Stevens's pedagogy. An anonymous former student who had later become a teacher wrote to Miss Stevens's sister Alice when she heard about Clara's death. This anonymous woman's comments reveal not only a picture of Stevens's classroom but also the lasting impact they had:

> I think no one who was ever in her classes can forget her sympathy and understanding, and her marvelous ability in taking the contributions of her students, poor and feeble as they often were, and making of them something vital and worth while. I am sure hundreds of her pupils all over the world now engaged in the work of teaching, as I am, have almost daily cause to bless her for what she taught them about the work of teaching. (Cheek, Warbeke and Griffith 228)

Stevens's patience with her students, her ability to help them work through "poor and feeble" contributions in order to reach a final vital product was ultimately a lesson to the students who would later become teachers themselves. Cheek, Warbeke, and Griffith's memorial collection also includes brief material from four other former students who echo Miss Stevens's ability to make much of class time, to encourage students to be clear and express themselves well, and to befriend her students.

In many ways, the descriptions of Stevens's classroom above echo Ira Shor's words about the liberatory learning process, and about the ways liberatory learning spaces must be defined. Shor articulates the critical classroom as follows:

> The teacher needs to come to class with an agenda, but must be ready for anything, committed to letting go when the discussion is searching for an organic form. [. . .] Down from the pedestal and out from behind the lectern, the teacher leaves behind the simplicity of lectures and term papers for something much more rigorous and compelling. (101–102)

Instead of "manipulated objects," students become "active, critical subjects" in such a forum (95). This form of teaching is evident in Stevens's classroom. The allowance for student voice and the active discussion would have led to much more difficult teaching for Stevens (as for any teacher) than if she had simply lectured. However, her commitment to students as knowing subjects would have helped her to reject a lecture-based format in favor of a more progressive and liberatory one. She obviously believed in her students as active constructors of knowledge and helped them work out such knowledge(s) for themselves.

In fact, much as Stevens had been trained to become a teacher under a progressive instructor like Scott, she too became involved in teacher training at Mount Holyoke. The papers of Ruth Johnson, Class of 1909, include her notebook from "Senior English," a teacher training course taken with Miss Stevens. The notes are a mix of advice on teaching writing and teaching literature, and include a fair number of lectures from guest speakers, the majority of whom were from local high schools. There are a number of suggestions for paper topics for students studying literature, as well as suggestions for teaching writing well. The notebook has several recommendations for textbooks, including those written by Carpenter, George P. Baker, and Scott, and Scott and Denney's *Elementary Composition*. There are many student-centered suggestions that Stevens recommends to her pupils, including "philosophy of the Assignment—subject *must* be interesting to teacher as well as pupil," and "base questions on pupils' own knowledge. Question of comparison," and "Ask him one question that will make him *think*." Stevens also recommends letting students correct their own work and "lay stress on securing image"—in other words, capturing ideas rather than dwelling on sentences as they drafted. Stevens also offered a list of questions for her students to ask as they were visiting schools, which not only reflects her views about teaching but also about English's relationship to other disciplines. The questions include time spent on paper revision, methods used to teach grammar ("can it be made interesting?"), and the cooperation of other departments in creating standards for written work in English.

Most importantly, Stevens's sense that students should own their own writing and derive power from it can be seen in her advice to future teachers. Ruth Johnson's notebook comments almost immediately on the reputation writing has for most students and the fact that good teachers must work to reverse it. They must instead help the student see the power of knowledge inherent in writing. Johnson writes, "Inspire pupils—Inherited hatred for word 'composition.' Take the word and show its meaning. Show we are always composing—always talking. World full of interesting subject to write and talk about. Question not-'What shall I say?' but 'What do I know?'" While Johnson's notes are obviously disjointed, they offer a sense of Stevens's own views even as she offers advice for teaching others. These words might have been written by Fred Newton Scott himself; they are certainly in keeping with Progressive Era views about student work and the ability of students, as well as helping students find interesting topics to write about and engaging them as active and participatory learners.

Stevens also believed, much like Scott and Dewey, that education could provide students with powerful voices that could be used within their own environments. Stevens clearly indicates in her scholarship that teaching students to write and to speak well was to teach them to have power. As quoted earlier from "College English" (in her opening paragraph, no less), she notes that "[. . .] college courses in writing should go far toward making our college graduates men and women of abounding and at the same time controlled life, and men and women of power" (101). Particularly during the Progressive Era, when individuals saw themselves as individual and group agents for social change, such power was an important part of college education and life. While Stevens does not overtly mention that this power could be used publicly for their participation in a democracy, her implication to this effect is clear.

Stevens also believed connections to the personal could help students enter conversations and therefore feel as if they have powerful positions from which to speak. She in fact spends the second half of "College English" discussing ways to help students make personal connections with the literature they are reading, and in turn write about those. She also expounds on the idea of having classes discuss topics before they wrote about them and allowing a pre-writing and connection stage that helped them gain a position of strength and authority before they began writing. With this model, students also often had the option for multiple revisions, allowing them more opportunities to control the direction of their work. All of these factors were used with the idea of students gaining power over their own words. For Stevens, there was no clear reason for a division between personal and academic—they were interconnected and needed to be used with one another in order to give the student power in expression: "overcoming difficulties, giving at last clear and adequate expression to his experience, the student has a sense of mastery, of power. This power will be increased in a series of actions and reactions" (101). The constant, cyclical nature of gathering thoughts and ideas, relating them to what a person already knows, and working to express them in an organized way, ultimately blends the academic and personal so that there cannot be a clear division. The academic becomes personal, the personal academic, and both are dependent on a series of Deweyian transactions.

More fully articulated support for Stevens's Deweyian pedagogy of inclusion and active learning can be found in her 1906 article "College English." Throughout the article she states her views on how students can obtain power through knowledge and writing, and reasons why teachers should avoid standardized methods of instruction. She herself declares that she prefers to avoid discussing her method of teaching, but instead offers this advice:

> In general it may be said that any method will make for power which incites a student to study a subject rather than an assigned lesson. Any method is good which makes a student do his best work,—hard work it may be, and should be, but satisfying. Any method is good which makes a student think and adequately voice his thought. (105)

Stevens required multiple drafts of her students' writing, and her style of teaching indicates that she valued the learning process as much as she did the final acquisition of certain knowledge. It is obvious, as well, that she did value writing as a skill, and a necessary skill for the job market and life.

Stevens's actions and her relationships also invoked Deweyian ideas, including the rejection of binaries. In particular, she worked to avoid the professor/student binary. Instead, she functioned as mother-teacher rather than a professor in the most formal sense. Stevens lived in the single dorm that Mount Holyoke had when she first began teaching there, and she was remembered for organizing a reading circle that met in her room on Tuesday nights (Cheek, Warbeke, and Griffith 222). She was also put in charge of Safford Hall when it was built in 1897 (faculty often served as early house mothers), and lived there for seven years. Even once she moved off campus when she and sister Alice Stevens, also a faculty member, built a house across the street from the college, she invited other faculty members to live in their home. Her physical removal from the college, however, did not create a separation from the close relationship she had with her students. Former colleague

Helen Griffiths, who lived with the sisters when she first began teaching at the college, remembered the connection Stevens created. "Her tea table was set out every Monday afternoon. Around it met town and gown, faculty and students. On Sunday afternoons, also, her friends often gathered around the hearth fire for talk. English majors, two by two, were entertained at Sunday night supper" (Cheek, Warbeke, and Griffith 226). Stevens made her personal and close relationships with her students a priority, even as their professor.

This breakdown in professor/student relationships can also be seen in the memorial tributes about Stevens. While there is no overt discussion of a maternal role toward her students, memoirs and memorial tributes reflect on her personality, using key phrases such as *warm personality* and *mature wisdom*. Griffith comments that "what most of us remember first about Miss Stevens is the warm, outgoing interest she took in her students and friends and in everything that concerned them. She was an ideal repository for confidences" (226). A former student also noted that Stevens was "so interested in us all, so keenly alive to world interests as well as our personal interests, so self-forgetful" (228). Stevens clearly had developed a complex understanding of the student-teacher relationship and used this to nurture and foster such relationships. She was used to close student-teacher relationships from her own undergraduate and graduate experiences, and she modeled collegiate but close relationships for her students.

Stevens's commitment to the department in its most crucial developing years is also clear. Through her progressive instruction, she also had the interest of the students at heart, helping them become contributing members of their society, either through the ability to think clearly and create powerful prose, or as teachers or scholars. Stevens's vision was closer to today's beliefs about supportive experiential learning than it was to the views of the majority of her peers. In fact, her methods created a drastically different classroom than the influences in all-male settings and the violence against the professors Connors describes ("Woman's Reclamation" 73). Connors notes that rhetoric was often "intensely agonistic," and the presentations college boys were to give were publicly (and often extremely nastily) criticized. Faculty members were harsh and critical; students often openly rebelled and even physically attacked professors on occasion. Connors links the violence on college campuses to the study of rhetoric, which taught verbal attack and counter-attack. As rhetoric began to change, however, and co-educational atmospheres diminished fraternity-like behavior, so too the agonistic atmosphere of the rhetoric classroom became less hostile and violent (*Composition-Rhetoric* 48). Violence, antagonism, skill drill and extreme structure were not part of Stevens's pedagogy. The result of a combination of her progressive training and the all-women's atmosphere, Stevens's classroom operated on a much less agonistic scale. She was a model to be emulated; her department was designed and later operated after her own model.

Stevens, of course, would not have described her teaching methods as "feminist." However, her teaching indeed fits modern descriptions for feminist pedagogy. Linda Markowitz presents three components of feminist pedagogy intended to help students critique binaries and examine knowledge construction: "These are participatory learning, social construction of knowledge and the legitimation of personal experience" (42). Stevens's work shows her commitment to student experience, her constant work to help students understand the basis for their knowledge and how to derive power from it, and her participation in a teaching-learning environment. Markowitz, writing about the goals for feminist pedagogy one hundred years after Stevens wrote about effective composition pedagogy, sounds remarkably like Stevens when she comments that "it is precisely because we ask students to become aware of how and why they possess their knowledge claims that they become cognizant of their power to create, shape, and change knowledge" (42). Stevens was pursuing the same goals in 1900 for her students, under the guise of progressivist pedagogy, that Markowitz pursued for her students in 2005 under the guise of feminist pedagogy.

Later in Stevens's career at Mount Holyoke, she continued to focus on writing instruction. In fact, she worked with other departments within the school to discuss writing instruction and to assess need. While the burden of responsibility for writing instruction was located in the English department, Stevens advocated cooperation between the departments on the issue. A *Questionnaire*, distributed in 1922 when Stevens was still working in a part-time capacity for the department, shows her concern for issues regarding writing and is a clear precursor to the Writing Across the Curriculum/Writing in the Disciplines initiatives of today. It assesses information literacy, organization and coherence, use of personal voice, matters of syntax, and possibilities for interdepartmental collaboration and cooperation. It is worth reproducing here in its entirety.

Questionnaire

Please return to Miss Stevens by February 22.

I. What tools do you expect students to be able to use when they enter your classes? e.g.
  1. Do you expect them to know the relative value of the standard dictionaries and encyclopedias?

      To work up their own bibliographies?
      To make out regular bibliography cards for the references consulted? Anything else?

  2. Do you think that methods of note-taking should be taught, or should they be found out by each student for herself?

      What instruction, if any, do you give about note-taking?

  3. Do you expect them to be able to present the results of their reading in organized written form?

      Do you expect these papers to show selected reproduction of the reading, or a more personal assimilation of it by the student?
      Do you expect independent organization in these papers, or is a student at liberty to borrow a plan she has found in her reading?
      Do you expect references to be given for all indebtedness whatsoever, whether of fact or of opinion?
      How would you like to have the references indicated?
      Do you expect bibliographies with these papers? What do you require in addition to title and author?

II. What are the chief complaints you have to make of the papers that students hand in to you?
      In general appearance and form?
      In use of material from their reading?
      In matters of expression?
      How general do you find deficiencies in these respects among your students?

III. Do you consider matters of English in grading your papers?
      How do you treat illiterate English in papers prepared outside of this class?
      How do you treat misspelling?

How do you treat plagiarism?

IV. Have you any suggestions for more effective cooperation between the English department and other departments? (English Department Papers)

The results of the survey were also made available in conference notes from the 1922 Intercollegiate English Conference, which involved Mount Holyoke, Vassar, Smith, and Wellesley (see Mastrangelo and L'Eplattenier). The report from the conference indicates that such a survey was conducted at the other schools as well, and results were tabulated. Many of the comments provided are not dissimilar to comments produced from departments outside of English today, and include the following often contradictory statements:

> In each college represented, whenever reports and papers are written for other departments, certain specific criticisms filter through to the English department. Some of these criticisms we briefly tabulate, arranging them in pairs, so that the occasional conflict of ideals may be apparent.
>
> Students are unable to sustain their thought through a paper of any length.
>
> Students are unable to condense their thought to a paper of any brevity.
>
> Students are not trained to handle material gained from books with any originality.
>
> Students cannot handle material gained from books in an accurate, straightforward way; they attempt to adorn it with literary conceits and to attack it in some "original" fashion.
>
> Students employ a baffling form of plagiarism, presenting without acknowledgement opinions quoted from authors read.
>
> Students have been trained to be too trivial about giving authorities for opinions borrowed. They speckle their pages with references.
>
> Students cannot write in logical form with a definite outline.

> Students have been overtrained in the conventional outline form; they warp their material for the sake of neat tabulation.
>
> Illiterate English persists in senior letters and papers. (English Department Papers)

The initiation of such a survey on Stevens's part indicates a dedication to writing instruction, and a commitment to try to address the overall writing needs of students, both inside and outside the department itself. It also demonstrates Stevens's Deweyian idea of making connections, both with the students and with other departments. Her reaching out to other departments meant she was aware of "complaints" and difficulties with student writing, and was working to improve the work of the students.

One difficulty with both the survey and the results is that the definition of *illiterate* English is lost to the modern reader because of the deictic nature of literacy. While current definitions involve discussions of functional literacy (i.e., a person can read and write enough to manage daily tasks), it is likely that the definition of illiteracy Stevens uses in her survey has more to do with students who were using grammatically and syntactically suspect language with multiple usage errors. In any case, the survey shows the effort on the part of Stevens and her colleagues to make connections between their work and the work of the other departments, both at Mount Holyoke and other colleges as well. The results tabulated echo the Harvard Reports, and show the extent to which pervasive negative views of writing prevailed at colleges and universities even in the 1920s. The results also mirror many modern sentiments regarding writing instruction (Sheils's "Why Johnny Can't Write," in the 1975 *Newsweek*, for example), some of which even come from departments of English themselves. Recently, compositionists have regarded such dominant responses to student writing as coming from those who did not understand student error in texts (see Flower and Hayes and Shaugnessey, among others), and were working from current-traditionalist assumptions that student mistakes were the result of a deficit in the students' knowledge and ability, rather than a structural or patterned difficulty, lack of experience, or even a flaw in the writing assignment. Stevens's views on student writing are much closer to recent ones. Her overall influence at Mount Holyoke seems to have kept some of the current-traditionalism that surrounded her at bay, and it is obvious based on the yearly meetings of an intercollegiate English conference that she attempted to work with other progressive pedagogues as well (see Mastrangelo and L'Eplattenier).

While Stevens was a dominant force behind the teaching of writing at Mount Holyoke, she also maintained a collegial and cooperative attitude with those teaching literature. At the same time that Mary Lyon and those who followed in her footsteps valued rhetoric (including its written form), literature was a distinctly separate component of education for Mount Holyoke students. Under Clara Stevens's direction, the English department (which focused on writing and rhetorical study) at Mount Holyoke continued to flourish and included literary criticism, which would have been much more focused on a critique of various styles and structures of writing than is thought of today. At the same time, the Department of English Literature, a separate entity from the Department of English, was also present. The two disciplines, one stressing writing and the other the study of literature, did not service enough students to be in conflict with one another. They had originally developed as separate departments in 1897, when departmentalization was at its peak at Mount Holyoke (Cheek, Warbeke, and Griffith 223). While the two were very different places in terms of their curriculum, the department notes and student journals evidence no hostility toward one another. There seems to have been a recognition that they were there to accomplish different goals, and they were amicable in achieving them. There continued to be writing exercises assigned in English Literature classes, as well as readings in the English classes. Such a coexistence was no doubt largely thanks to Stevens and her continued emphasis on the importance of writing instruction at the college level. At the same time that Stevens supported writing instruction, she also encouraged professors trained in literature to teach in her department, and seems to have worked hard not to denigrate the study of literature. Her writing, in fact, reflects a use of literary texts in the writing classroom. Many faculty as well were listed as teaching in both departments until the Department of English, encompassing both literature and rhetoric, was formed in 1947.

MOUNT HOLYOKE'S ENGLISH DEPARTMENT, POST-STEVENS

Clara Stevens officially retired from Mount Holyoke College in 1921 and died in 1934. For some time after her retirement and death, the

English department continued in much the same vein. Adaline Potter, who graduated from Mount Holyoke in 1931 and taught at Mount Holyoke in a part-time capacity from 1948 to 1975, remembers her experiences as an English major. While Potter was a student, Stevens's continued influence in the department is clear in Potter's descriptions of her classes. Discussion was encouraged in Potter's classes, and multiple drafts of papers were required. Potter also recalled that the English Department, with its concentration on writing instruction, was considered more rigorous than the Department of English Literature. "A's" were very difficult to come by, even for excellent students, and students in the English Department were encouraged to be scholars rather than just "nice, educated girls." Potter felt that the strict discipline in the department and the difficult work challenged her to work even harder.

Despite continued emphasis on the part of some faculty for progressive teaching methods, major changes in English studies occurred after Stevens's retirement and death. In 1937, Roswell Ham was appointed as president of Mount Holyoke College, succeeding Mary Woolley. Ham was the college's president from 1937 to 1957, and was inaugurated in the college's centennial year. Ham was Mount Holyoke's first male president, and his appointment met with considerable resistance from alumnae, many of whom felt that a woman should continue the presidency of the college. Ham's presence was not an especially welcome one, and his English background from Yale, where he completed his PhD in English Literature in 1925, made his interest in English studies especially intense. His concentration was in English tragic drama, and in addition to his duties as president of Mount Holyoke, he taught courses in English Literature and Shakespeare (Personal Papers). Cyrus Northrup, in his 1902 *Report of the Commissioner of Education*, noted that most Yale-trained educators "have had on them all their lives the stamp of Yale College, and have cherished the Yale ideas and have followed the Yale methods. No other single word describes what these are so well as 'conservatism'" (589–590).[8] Indeed, Ham's idea for the improvement of the English studies program at Mount Holyoke included merging the Department of English and the Department of English Literature. Economically, of course, this would have made sense in the midst of the Great Depression and the beginning of World War II, when the college was facing potential financial difficulties. The college was also concerned about its image at this time, and was motivated to update numerous programs (including the architecture on campus) in order to remain cutting edge. However, Ham's idea was actually regressive. Departmental memos indicate that Ham was not inclined to think highly of writing instruction, was not inclined to leave the two departments as they were, and would eventually see to it that they were combined. By his second year of office (1938), Ham was already asking the two departments to come up with plans for consolidation.

The two departments at Mount Holyoke initially fought Ham's decision. Both departments felt that they had worked well side by side for nearly fifty years, and that there was no need to change. As of 1942, under much duress, the two departments somewhat hesitantly agreed to operate as one under a divisional system with one administration and one chair position. Professors were to advise students in their own subject area, and students were required to take courses in both divisions. Division I incorporated the English Department (writing instruction and rhetorical theory), and Division II incorporated the Department of English Literature. The entire department became the Department of English Language and Literature by 1947, eventually shortened again to the Department of English.

Eventually, after much debate over teaching loads and course designations, the department did reach resolution. In the process, courses that seemed to overlap at all were eliminated, and instructors were reassigned. It is not clear whether the Division II faculty had much to do with writing instruction, but it is likely they did not. Eventually, many of the well-established, long-standing composition-rhetoric courses were phased out. Stevens's course in debate was voted out in 1945, and the requirements for the major were merged so that the major divisions within the department were not so obvious.[9] One united department was eventually formed, at least on paper. Adaline Potter noted that the system worked well while she worked there, and she attributed its success to the collegiality of the faculty. She also noted that the arrangement was similar to the system Smith College used at that time.

Writing instruction in its various forms has always been present at Mount Holyoke, and it is possible to critically imagine what this might have looked like by examining the existing documents. From these documents, it is clear Mary Lyon and the students who later studied and taught at the institution were keenly aware of the need for women to be versed in the art of rhetoric (both as oral and written persuasion) in order to succeed in the world they inhabited, although in some cases this may have backfired as Mount Holyoke's graduates tried to reconcile their newfound knowledge with a society that often required their public silence.

Early education at Mount Holyoke, as this chapter has shown, was fairly progressive overall. In keeping with the cycles of education, however, Lyon's successors moved to a more current-traditional model. While this would have kept the college contemporary in its pedagogy, it would have done so to the detriment of Lyon's original progressive vision. When the educational system as a whole experienced the influences of Deweyian progressivism, so too did Mount Holyoke's English Department. Stevens's approach to writing instruction, which was part of the larger Progressive Movement influenced by Dewey and Scott, recovered and added to Lyon's original progressive beliefs. As the rest of the country became involved in more conservative practices in the 1930s and 1940s, so too did Mount Holyoke's English department. By 1925, just four years after Stevens's retirement, part of this shift is evident. In department meeting minutes from October 6, 1925, discussion centered around "the aims for freshman work" and several questions were raised. These included some about recruiting for the English major through the first-year course. In addition to these, however, question number two was raised: "should there be an attempt to adapt freshman work to the individual?" This would have seemed an odd question twenty years (or even ten) earlier, when *all* work was adapted to the individual. Current-traditionalism, by then rampant in English departments across the country, eventually found a stronghold in the Mount Holyoke English department as well. Despite the thirty-year progressive respite Stevens provided, writing instruction eventually assumed the place it continues to hold today at many institutions—absorbed and bested by literature.

In conclusion, rhetoric at Mount Holyoke allows a window through which to view the historical movement of rhetoric in the educational system of the United States. While composition-rhetoric has always been present at Mount Holyoke, its development was subject to the same ebbs and tides of change that education as a whole experienced throughout the one hundred years this chapter surveys. While the pedagogy of those such as Stevens helped her maintain an entire department of rhetoric, after she left, the department was absorbed by an English department that included studies of both literature and composition/rhetoric. Lyon and Stevens were certainly among the personalities who sought to actively change the historical role of composition-rhetoric, and to locate a place within rhetoric's multiple definitions for both an active pedagogy and the discourse of women.

Stevens's knowledge, innovative teaching, continual work towards improvement of writing instruction, and overall spirit should not be forgotten as contemporary compositionists work to recover the history of writing instruction. Stevens's progressivism, defined through her active and critical pedagogy and student-centered learning, created a Dewyian progressive classroom Dewey himself would have been proud of. As historians seek to recover Deweyian progressivism, and compositionists specifically work to create innovative, critical approaches to the teaching of writing, they would do well to familiarize themselves with Clara Frances Stevens.

4 Sophie Chantal Hart and Wellesley College

> *It is not too sweeping to assert that Wellesley's development and academic standing are due to the cooperative wisdom and devoted scholarship of her faculty. The initiative has been theirs. They have proved that a college for women can be successfully taught and administered by women. To them Wellesley owes her academic status.*
>
> —Florence Converse

> *How shall we divide one into three and make each third equal to a whole? How shall the same individual devote herself effectively to the three vocations of woman, teacher, and scholar? For it is still a profession in itself to be a woman. . . . We may calculate eclipses, but we are not set free from the tyranny of the needle. Even blue stockings have to be darned.*
>
> —Katherine Lee Bates

In researching and critically imagining Clara Stevens and the Mount Holyoke English department, I began to wonder if Stevens was perhaps a lone figure, an anomalous and solitary progressive woman teaching English. Was it possible to create a story of social circulation for her? To imagine her in conversation with others who believed and taught in similar ways under similar circumstances? When I came across the minutes for the 1919 Intercollege Conference on English Composition, held at Mount Holyoke, I saw that Stevens had interacted with several other women who were also a part of the progressive tradition. As I viewed documents from the Intercollege Conference, names like Gertrude Buck from Vassar, Mary Augusta Jordan from

Smith College, and Sophie Chantal Hart of Wellesley were on the list of participants. Curious about Hart, since I had never particularly heard of her, I began to look for other references to her. Like my work with Stevens, I worked to critically imagine Hart in her surroundings, using, as Kirsch and Royster call for, "fragments woven together to create a narrative, a theory, a history, a better understanding of women's lived experiences, past and present" (640).

Because I had already completed my work on Stevens before I researched Hart, I was better able to see Hart contextually in ways that had been more difficult with my work with Stevens. I was able to imagine Hart's interactions with women from other colleges and see the ways Deweyian pedagogy had gained social circulation, especially amongst Scott's former students and the women they taught. I had to work much harder to critically imagine Hart, but some factual evidence does exist from which to start. Hart, unlike Stevens, was not a graduate of Wellesley returning to her alma mater to teach. Instead, she graduated from Radcliffe in 1892 and was immediately hired to teach at Wellesley. Eventually I discovered she and Clara Stevens actually had quite a bit in common. Hart pursued her master's at Michigan (completed in 1898) in the same program Stevens had attended. Hart then returned to work at Wellesley, teaching in the department for an impressive forty-five years, thirty-eight of which she was chair. Hart, like Stevens, espoused progressive pedagogies and encouraged her student writers in progressive ways. Hart's work within the department makes her a critical part of the history of the department and the history of progressive educational practices at Wellesley.

It is important to develop an understanding of Hart's surroundings at Wellesley in order to better contextualize and critically imagine her within them. Discussions of Wellesley College's departmental history as a whole, as well as of the English department specifically, are difficult for a variety of reasons. First, no official or unofficial history of the department exists the way one does for Mount Holyoke College, leaving me to extrapolate from college histories and other documents that mention English studies, but do not focus on them. Second, a fire in 1914 destroyed a majority of the college's archival records, limiting early archival evidence. The English department lost all of its offices and books, as well as all of its records. As a result, historical work must focus on remaining records, documents donated by alumnae and relatives of alumnae since the fire, and written accounts that were housed outside of the structures that burned. The few records that do exist (primarily in the form of President's Annual Reports and College Catalogs) show a somewhat confusing history of the departmentalization of English studies. It seems that as early as 1889, there were two departments in existence. These included a Department of English Language and Rhetoric and a Department of English Language. By 1906–1907, department records indicate three divisions: a Department of English Literature, a Department of English Language, and a Department of Composition, all under a general heading of English. The English Language department, according to the 1909 President's Annual Report, was comprised of the linguistics-based courses such as Old English that had previously been offered in the other two departments. By 1925, English Literature absorbed English Language, and by 1947, the remaining two departments had combined into a single English department.

In addition to the limited archival information, discussions of English studies in other sources are also relatively scarce. Florence Converse, writing about Wellesley's history, has very little to say about any of the English Studies departments in either *The Story of Wellesley* (1915) or *Wellesley College: A Chronicle of the Years 1875–1938* (1939). References to the departments are discussed merely in terms of their faculty members, and little is said regarding the overall structures or course offerings. However, more recent research regarding Wellesley's general history offers valuable information. Feminist historian Patricia Palmieri, for example, has done extensive work on Wellesley, its founding, its political activism, and especially its faculty. Again, while Palmieri has not focused specifically on English department activity, her work provides a general view of Wellesley and a sense of some of the English faculty members that helps contribute to an understanding of the history of a single department. Other sources include Katherine Lee Bates's essay on composition studies at Wellesley, published in *The Dial* in 1894 and included in William Morton Payne's 1895 collection of *English in American Universities*. Bates's essay seems to be the only one in existence that fully profiles the early Wellesley English department, and helps communicate a greater understanding of the overall purpose and general teaching philosophy underlying the practical matter of teaching writing. Lastly, but not any less important, archival papers do exist that attest to the existence of progressive pedagogues at Wellesley.

One of the most notable but least recognized teachers whose papers are housed in the archives is Sophie Chantal Hart. Hart's archival papers, including letters and transcriptions of the Intercollege Conference on English in which she took part (along with Clara Stevens), allow modern readers to critically imagine a progressive pedagogue whose life's work was her teaching. Little evidence of Hart's work specifically at Wellesley exists. To fail to extrapolate from existing sources would be to maintain the silence that currently exists regarding her work. However, discussions of Hart are often comprised of conjecture and projection as a result. Kirsch and Royster's notion of strategic contemplation is especially important here, because critical imagining can only go so far. As Kirsch and Royster point out, strategic contemplation is often "an important step in scholarly productivity, especially when traditional, more publicly rendered sources of information are in short supply, as is often the case with the documentation of women's experience" (656). Part of my contemplation of Hart, then, is informed by her social and historical context and my knowledge of what it meant for her to be trained in Fred Newton Scott's graduate program and to teach at a turn-of-the century women's college.

As previously noted, some documents do exist that help me imagine Hart more fully. Born in California in 1868, Hart was sixteen when she left California and entered Radcliffe. She graduated from Radcliffe in 1892, after having spent part of her sophomore year observing Toynbee Hall in London as well as other progressive municipal housing projects (Chappell 183). She later returned to visit college settlements and the board schools. Later in life, Hart spent sabbatical time in China, England, and India, even lecturing for a month in Constantinople (Chappell 183). She was involved in national and international progressive associations. She was an early female member of the Modern Language Association, "director of the North Atlantic Section of the American Association of University Women and a member of the National Fellowship Award committee and of the National Board of Foreign Relations committee, and one of five voting delegates of the International Federation of University Women" (Chappell 183). She was clearly interested and invested in Progressive Era concerns, particularly those involving education and women.

Hart's life's work, in essence, was her students, and her primary concern, like Stevens's, was the teaching of writing. As a result, Hart published little, and only one piece appeared in a scholarly journal.

Hart published "English in the Colleges" in 1902 in *The School Review*. Her views on teaching can also be seen in "English Composition—An Interpretation," a reflective piece written at the time of her retirement and published in the *Wellesley Magazine*. As well, multiple memorial tributes exist that reveal the nature of her teaching.[1] Supplemental letters, department memos, and conference proceedings help complete a recreation of Hart's pedagogy. Preceding any discussion of Hart, however, a brief overview of the history of the founding of Wellesley, as well as a history of the development of English studies at the college, can help properly frame the context for Sophie Chantal Hart's work while at the college.

THE HISTORY OF WELLESLEY

Wellesley College's history starts somewhat later than many of the other women's seminaries, such as Mount Holyoke or Emma Willard. Opened in 1875, Wellesley was in the middle of the births of the Seven Sisters. By the time Wellesley opened in 1875, Mount Holyoke (seminary in 1837, college in 1888) and Vassar (1865) were already in existence. Smith (1875) opened its doors concurrently. Barnard, Bryn Mawr, and Radcliffe would open later. Wellesley opened its doors in 1875 as a fully endowed college, located on the estate of Henry Fowle Durant. Durant had some simple but crucial advantages over the founders of other colleges in the nineteenth century. Working relatively late in the century, he was able to use the already founded institutions as role models. These colleges offered Durant both social and educational models from which to work. He also had extensive financial resources, which meant the college did not need to fundraise immediately.

It was in fact through the ministry that Durant became so involved with the issue of women's education. An Evangelical preacher, during the 1860s he gave occasional sermons at Mount Holyoke, staying for several days at a time in order to counsel the young women (Horowitz 43). By 1867, Durant had been made a trustee of Mount Holyoke. As such, he was well-connected and well-educated regarding issues of women's colleges. The influence of Mount Holyoke on Durant is clear in his statement, "there can never be too many Mount Holyokes" (Stow 239; Woody, Volume II, 149). Durant's notions of *why* women should be educated, however, were far different from Mary Lyon's.

Durant was much more of a political activist than Lyon had been, and he believed women could contribute more to society if they were freed from its constraints, rather than learning to live within them. According to Thomas Woody, Durant "was, moreover, convinced that social questions of the future could not be answered save by the assistance of enlightened women" (Volume II, 149). In a sermon, he proclaimed:

> We revolt against the slavery in which women are held by the customs of society—the broken health, the aimless lives, the subordinate position, the helpless dependence, the dishonesties and shams of so-called education. The Higher Education of Women . . . is the cry of the oppressed slave. It is the assertion of absolute equality . . . it is the war of Christ . . . against spiritual wickedness in high places. (Horowitz 44)

Durant was joined in his mission to educate women by his wife, Pauline. Both Henry and Pauline Durant believed women should have educational opportunities available to them. As a result, they abandoned an original plan to leave their money for the creation of an orphanage, and instead decided in the late 1860s to create a model of women's education of their own. They petitioned the Massachusetts legislature for the formation of a seminary. Notably, they differed from Mount Holyoke in one respect: while men were involved with the board of trustees, so too were women, including Pauline Durant (Palmieri, *In Adamless Eden* 9).[2] By 1873, the Durants had changed their minds regarding the mission of the institution, and they re-petitioned, this time to begin a college.

Durant recruited his all-female faculty for Wellesley from places like Mount Holyoke, Oberlin, Vassar, Columbia, Yale, and Michigan. When he realized the overall difficulty (and impracticality) of recruiting thirty qualified women, he instead began recruiting good teachers, even from high schools, and paying for them to be trained for college level teaching (Horowitz 54). While such an investment seems on the surface to be unsound fiscal and educational practice, in truth it allowed Durant not only to have trained teachers but to ensure they were trained under his close supervision. Because many of Durant's instructors were trained at cutting-edge institutions such as the University of Michigan, they were exposed to progressivist methods of instruction and training, which they brought back with them to their Wellesley classrooms. This practice meant that in later years, Wellesley's faculty had fewer advanced degrees among the more established faculty than at peer institutions. In 1915, for example, only 25% of Wellesley's full professors had a PhD, compared to 80% at Smith and Vassar (Dealey 348). However, because women who began teaching careers later had greater opportunities for higher education, over 50% of the assistant professors at Wellesley had PhDs, a number comparable to Smith and Vassar (Dealey 348).

Changes in administration came about at Wellesley just after its opening. Durant himself was not young when he founded the college, and he died in 1881, only six years after the college opened. The president at the time, Ada Howard, was herself ill. In November of 1881, Howard was asked to step down, and Alice Freeman (later Alice Freeman Palmer), a Michigan graduate and Professor of History, was asked to take the next presidency (Palmieri, *In Adamless Eden* 17). Freeman's appointment was somewhat of a surprise, as she was one of the younger members of the faculty. At the age of twenty-six, her responsibilities were daunting. Freeman worked to enhance the faculty while at the same time attempting to retain the spirit of Wellesley that Durant had created, raising salaries and recruiting young progressive scholars (Palmieri, *In Adamless Eden* 36). Freeman also promoted women's education at the secondary level as she worked to help establish secondary schools that would ensure the development of students who were academically prepared for a women's college. According to Palmieri, Freeman helped open high quality secondary schools in Wellesley and Auburndale (both in Massachusetts), Chicago, New York City, Kansas City, and Philadelphia (*In Adamless Eden* 31). Freeman's influence on others regarding the importance of women's education very well may have kept Wellesley (as well as some of her sister schools) alive in the early years.

Freeman was also influential in combining women's education with social service to the community. Following the likes of Catherine Beecher, who believed in the force of women in the classroom, Freeman added a progressivist theory of social involvement. She believed women should be involved in social and moral reform causes. Working with the progressive belief that everyone should have access to education, Freeman "saw [women] as important to public life and in the 1880s advanced the belief that college-trained women teachers were significant to the progressive civilization of America" (Palmieri 31–32). While the goal of a progressive civilization was typical of the time, Freeman's idea of using women as teachers to attain such a goal was relatively new during the 1880s, and while the concept of educating women in order that they could then educate their sons for participation in the democracy had already gained some merit, higher education for women was usually seen as unnecessary.

Freeman believed women could be, and should be, more than women, and more than teachers. As a result, she encouraged her faculty to be pedagogues in the truest sense of the word. She encouraged them to be teachers *and* scholars, and to consistently investigate the ways they did both. While Bliss Perry, in his 1897 article "The Life of a College Professor," indicated that there were two types of university professor, one who did research and one who taught, Freeman encouraged her faculty to be both. And while Perry felt that "sometimes it happens that the great teacher is also a great investigator, but that is a miracle," Freeman expected nothing less (514). The researcher who was not a good teacher as well had no place at Wellesley, nor did the teacher who never did research. Perry also indicated that "In one sense, indeed, [the professor] is supposed to know very little about the men he teaches" (516). Again, such was not the case at Wellesley. Perhaps it was Freeman's closeness in age to her students, perhaps it was the enactment of progressive forms of nurturing, perhaps it was Durant's original insistence on personal attention, but faculty at Wellesley lived and ate with their students in an unusually close environment, and knew their students extremely well on a personal level. The result is that part of the progressive pedagogy that was established at Wellesley invoked the Deweyian notion of establishing a close relationship between the teacher and student on multiple levels.

Progressive Pedagogy at Wellesley

Progressive pedagogy had early modeling at Wellesley, and the instructors were supportive of one another as less experienced faculty learned the ropes. Alice Freeman Palmer, as president of the college, was a role model for many of the other teachers. As Palmieri points out, "Freeman provided the academic women with precisely the blend of freedom and responsibility necessary to convert their intellectualism into significant, productive work. In the classroom, Freeman allowed her faculty complete freedom, giving them carte blanche in matters of curriculum and pedagogy and supporting experimentation and innovation in both" (*In Adamless Eden* 30). While Freeman's expertise was history, not English, she was a supporter of all academic subjects. She in fact worked to help the college create twelve divisions or departments and regularly met with department heads, giving them full permission for training or experimentation within their programs (Palmieri 30). Freeman's model of experimentation would have paved the way for people like Sophie Chantal Hart to be progressive within the English department, while the rest of the school also generally developed progressive goals and teaching strategies.

After Alice Freeman left Wellesley in 1886 to marry George Palmer (a professor at Harvard as well as a trustee of Wellesley), Helen Shafer was appointed as the new president. Shafer's work at Wellesley was of a different nature than Freeman's had been. According to Florence Converse, in *The Story of Wellesley*, "Miss Freeman's work we may characterize as, in its nature, extensive. Miss Shafer's was intensive. The scholar and administrator were united in her personality, but the scholar led" (76). Shafer's main work was to move the college closer to the German system, which was advocating a system that involved a core curriculum and then a selection of electives. Within five years in the 1890s, sixty-seven new courses were implemented, an unprecedented number for a college whose entire student body did not yet total five hundred undergraduates (Converse 78). By 1914–1915, the course catalog lists three hundred and twelve courses, addressing thirty-two subjects. English Composition was required for freshman, as were courses in Biblical History and Hygiene (Converse 132). Converse also indicates that the Academic Council was aware of the increasingly popular elective systems, and were working to keep the college's requirements competitive (133).

By the 1920s, Wellesley's progressive programs and faculty had attracted the attention of the rest of the country. Calvin Coolidge himself described Wellesley as a political "hotbed of radicalism" (Palmieri, *In Adamless Eden* xiv). It is easy to see why. Wellesley's women did not conform to the conventions of turn of the century America, which still typically demanded American women behave silently and respectfully, pursuing only those careers deemed suitable for women. While expectations were being raised regarding the educational levels of women, they were generally expected to be educated in order to be better wives and mothers rather than political activists and social reformers. While American women were expected to give back to their communities, helping to raise and educate children, the commitment of the Wellesley faculty to social change went beyond expectations. According to Palmieri's calculations in her work, "Here Was Fellowship: A Social Portrait of Academic Women at Wellesley College, 1895–1920," throughout their tenure at Wellesley, faculty involvement in reform activities was common. Out of fifty-three women who served on the faculty for five years or more, "39 (75 percent) were active in at least one of the following broad areas of reform: women's education and health reform; suffrage; social reform (temperance, consumer leagues, settlements, socialism, pacifism and opposition to tainted monies); and religious activism" (206). The faculty in English studies were no exception. Vida Scudder, for example, was a well-known social radical and literary theorist with her own FBI file. The English department as a whole supported and encouraged its students on their way to becoming public speakers, and offered classes in elocution, debate, and argumentation to prepare them.

English Studies at Wellesley

English studies at Wellesley had curious beginnings. Any very early history (1875–1890) is virtually unknown. Records do not indicate, beyond the listing of courses, what kinds of activities were going on during this time. Despite the lack of evidence, however, some extrapolation can be made from existing documents. Early writing instruction at Wellesley seems to have been very much like that at other co-educational institutions of the time. According to an 1875 table of course listings, freshman were required to take year-long courses in Elocution and Essay Writing, as were sophomores and juniors. Freshman were also required to take Modern English Literature, and sophomores studied History of Literature. By junior year, however, Rhetoric was also added to their study, although there is no description of exactly what this course entailed. The only English studies course required of the senior year was, again, Essay Writing (Palmieri, *In Adamless Eden* 12). While chroniclers such as Palmieri do not comment on Durant's influences in terms of writing instruction, it is clear that his model was based on comparable schools at the time. The inclusion of Elocution early in the college's curriculum also indicates a predisposition on his part to train women to be part of the speaking public, an unusual but not anomalous feature for a women's college.[3]

Unfortunately, not much detail exists as to exactly what Wellesley's early courses in English entailed. Presumably, they included essay writing in narration, description, and exposition, as were common for the time, as well as recitation, debate, and analysis of style. Records show that in 1889, the President's Annual Report lists a request for the development of a "journalistic germ" that would be run by the students. This move towards journalism would be connected to but separate from the rhetoric department. In 1889 as well, the President's Annual Report shows two departments—a department of English Language and Rhetoric, and one of English Literature.

Wellesley, like Mount Holyoke, was influenced by the movement in the late 1870s towards less belletristic and more rule-driven forms of teaching. Where other evidence is lacking, early listings of textbooks offer a way of understanding Wellesley's curriculum. While the use of any single text cannot suggest a particular teaching style, the collection of texts in use, gleaned from course catalogs and President's Annual Reports, offer an overall picture of a writing program that was relatively conservative prior to the arrival of Sophie Chantal Hart in the 1890s.

Prior to Hart's influence, details regarding the courses in rhetoric can be found in Wellesley's course catalog listings around 1890. Under Rhetoric there were three courses listed, presumably one for each of the freshman, sophomore, and junior years. The President's Annual Report lists the courses as follows:

> Course III. Lectures on English Prose Style. Analysis of Style, using Genung's Handbook, and Study of the Art of Fiction. Four Essays: four short papers.
>
> Course II. Argumentation and Oratory. Special attention given to debates written and spoken. Seven papers, including debates and essays.
>
> Course I. Structure of the Essay: Qualities of Style. Narration, Description, and Exposition. Study of models from Genung's Handbook. Six essays and frequent short papers. (President's Annual Report 1890)

Such descriptions connote a relatively traditional early program, at least in terms of writing instruction (here outlined in Courses I and III). As well, an 1890–1891 paper titled "Abbreviations Used in Correcting Essays" indicates that students should use Genung's *Practical Rhetoric* or Hill's "General Rules for Punctuation" as references for identifying and correcting errors. This mention of Genung matches the description of required materials provided in the President's Annual Report as well. Genung's text enjoyed great popularity in the United States in its time. His influence was wide, and the concentration in his book was on forms. Genung used the distinction of modes, including narration, description, exposition, argument, and persuasion (Kitzhaber 65). These modes were studied in Wellesley's courses as well, indicating that his textbook would have been a useful classroom tool.

In addition to the use of Genung, early course offerings at Wellesley list another text in particular that supports the fact that early English studies were rather conservative. Herbert Spencer's *The Philosophy of Style* (1852) was used early on in the department, as evidenced by the fact that extant exams ask students to evaluate materials using Spencer's text. Spencer himself was heavily invested in the change from a belletristic course of study to a more scientific one. Spencer saw the need for what he labeled a "rational" curriculum to take the place of the currently liberal arts-driven curriculum. As Joanne Wagner notes in her essay "'Intelligent Members or Restless Disturbers': Women's Rhetorical Styles, 1880–1920," Spencer's text was often used as a primary and secondary source in many women's colleges in the 1880s (187). Wagner surmises that the popularity of Spencer's text arises from a "simple psychological backing for his extremely prescriptive rules" (187). At a time when rhetorical study was being reduced to the rules of composition, and when the study of all subjects was being converted to scientific rather than subjective study, Spencer's text would have appealed to a large audience of teachers trying to make such a transition.

Adams Sherman Hill's *Principles of Rhetoric* was listed as an additional required text for early Wellesley students. It contained Hill's rules for punctuation, which Wellesley students were expected to follow. Hill's belief that other authors of literature should be used as examples "to illustrate how descriptive details can 'stimulate the imagination' is typical of the way in which nineteenth-century rhetoricians relied on a representative sampling of literary examples to demonstrate the skillful adaptation of rhetorical principles" (Johnson 82). Hill's influence to this end was extensive. Hill's *Principles of Rhetoric* seems to be listed as a staple text for the Wellesley rhetoric courses until at least 1935, where it appears on an extant syllabus. *Principles of Rhetoric* would have provided substantive commentary for students on correct forms of written expression.

Texts such as Hill, Genung, and Spencer were used at many institutions, including Harvard, during the later part of the nineteenth century. Again, while the use of these texts cannot offer windows into specific pedagogical practices, as a whole they indicate a relatively conservative approach to early writing instruction at Wellesley. Both the texts by Hill and Genung were standard staples for rhetoric courses across the United States; they are listed as primary texts adopted between 1875 and 1900 by a variety of institutions (Johnson 254).

In addition to standard writing courses, students studying at Wellesley did have access to another course that indicates their focus. In 1892, the English department offered a course in pedagogics, aimed specifically at those students who would go on to teach some time in their lives (which a majority of Wellesley's students did—an unprecedented seventy-one percent of the class of 1885 taught at some point during their lives, and an average of forty-two percent of graduates between 1879 and 1899 taught [Palmieri, *In Adamless Eden* 33]). The President's Annual Report of 1892 offers the following description of the course:

> Methods of work in the Kindergarten system and in primary, secondary, preparatory, and college grades are followed out in detail. Each student presents before the class several development lessons, one of which is oral. In this way the student's personal capacity as a teacher is brought out, and some opportunity is afforded her for putting into practice the theoretical knowledge previously gained. Representatives of different departments have kindly consented to give lectures, and thus a beginning has been made in the direction of supplementing general work in Pedagogics by a systematic introduction of special methods of teaching. (9)

It is interesting to note such a detailed description of a course in teacher training. It is also interesting to note that, like Mount Holyoke, it was located in the Wellesley English department, but that attempts were made to make it interdisciplinary. Not only would this have invoked Deweyian pedagogy on the level of training teachers to do specialized work but it also reflects Dewey's beliefs as it attempts to have students make connections between multiple disciplines and relate them back to the pursuit of teaching. Housing such a course in the English department is also reminiscent of the interest that composition retains today in matters of pedagogy. Composition tends to focus on pedagogy and examining a teacher's methods and motives, whereas many other subjects tend to retain a focus on developing expertise of subject matter. What is especially noteworthy about this course is that many of the instructors at Wellesley would have had very little teacher training themselves. Perhaps the pedagogics course was a defensive mechanism designed to help avoid some of the problems they had faced as they entered classrooms with a background in a particular subject area, but no knowledge of classroom practice.

Katherine Lee Bates, writing a description of the English department for an 1894 series of articles in *The Dial*, offers a glimpse into the increased numbers of students within the department and the struggle to accommodate them and teach them well. Bates's observations are worth reproducing here at length, as they indicate a predilection at Wellesley, as of 1894, for acontextual forms and formats rather than the contextualized and connected writing Fred Newton Scott espoused at the University of Michigan. Scott wished for a "laboratory model" for teaching students, where he envisioned workshop-based classes limited to a small number of students. Bates instead comments:

> Professor Scott's longed-for Utopia is not located at Wellesley. Frequent themes are required of the Freshmen, Sophomores, and Juniors, these classes numbering, in the aggregate, about six hundred. Moreover, here, as at Stanford and Indiana, classes of conditioned Freshmen are a conspicuous feature of the Rhetoric department, the training of the secondary schools being grievously inadequate. Miss Hart, of Radcliffe, and Miss Weaver . . . bend their united energies to developing in the Freshmen the ability to write clear, correct, well-constructed English sentences. To have mastered the paragraph is to become, so far as the Rhetoric department is concerned, a Sophomore; and to proceed . . . to the structure of the essay. (220)

Bates's observation about Michigan's influential program and Scott's views on the teaching of composition indicates that Bates was at least aware of more progressive programs than the one she was describing. In addition, Bates echoes contemporary arguments about inadequate secondary school instruction. It is difficult, however, to tell here exactly how writing was taught. While the idea that sentence mastery is the next step to paragraphs sounds fairly current-traditional, without teaching methods to back up the description it is difficult to be sure. Bates herself taught literature, and so her views may have been tainted as she was not trained in composition and rhetoric. Indeed, it bears asking why she was chosen to write the description for *The Dial* at all. Palmieri describes Bates's departmental leadership as one of "benevolent despotism," and this may have contributed to her description (122). In fact, in *The Dial* Bates laments the state of the instructors in rhetoric, noting that "it is unfortunate that they themselves are mortal, and have thus far been unable to accede to the desire of other Departments that all students whose technical themes and examination papers, while good in substance are bad in statement, shall be conditioned in English and turned over to the Rhetoric Department for reformation" (221). Bates's tone indicates that she had little use for the work involved in rhetoric, as long as it fixed the problems in writing that plagued other departments. In all, she views the rhetoric department as a service department, instead of a department with a fundamental theoretical and scholarly base for their work.

Bates's description seems to offer a current-traditional picture, but again, it is unclear overall how the early department at Wellesley functioned. The first comprehensive records of Wellesley's English studies begin to appear in the 1890s, making a much clearer critical imagining of Wellesley's English studies possible. It was during the early 1890s that English studies was to come under the leadership of two men from Harvard, who would have a large impact on the changes made at the time. While Durant had originally expressed a desire to retain an all-female faculty, for some reason the rhetoric department in the 1890s was placed under the leadership of George P. Baker and George Carpenter, both of Harvard. It is possible a dearth of qualified teachers forced the administration to temporarily hire the two men in order to keep the department functional. The courses were modeled after those at Harvard, and Brereton notes that the very presence of the likes of Baker in and of itself does not indicate a strong feminist program at Wellesley at this point. However, Baker was both an instructor at Radcliffe prior to this appointment, and was married to a Radcliffe alumna (Bordelon, "A Reassessment" 784).[4] Regardless of Baker's potential commitment to women's education, Wellesley certainly had its own instructors and potentially could have provided the instruction themselves, even if leadership was lacking (Brereton 183). In any case, through unknown circumstances, Baker and Carpenter were hired.

By 1893, shortly after the two men arrived at Wellesley, changes in the methods of instruction are visible. Wellesley's department, which previously did not indicate its particular model of imparting course information, began to model itself more after the Harvard model of lecture sections and discussion sections. The President's Report of 1893 notes, "the work in the Department of Rhetoric has been greatly changed through the introduction of new methods. In the new course for freshman, Mr. Carpenter has given through lectures a survey of the whole field" (16–17). While the lectures were delivered by Carpenter, Sophie Chantal Hart and a colleague, a Miss Weaver, were responsible for the smaller discussion-type sections where students apparently applied the lecture material to actual writing practice. By modern standards, Hart and Weaver functioned as many teaching assistants do today, doing the grunt work as professors who outranked them did the more scholarly work of imparting knowledge to be synthesized by students. Themes were presented once a week during the first semester, and once every two weeks during the second semester. Unbelievable as it may seem, Hart and Weaver were responsible for the theme writing of two hundred students apiece. Weaver, in addition, taught another twenty-six students in a course in Theme Writing (President's Report 1895). The huge number of students per instructor (although they were divided into seven discussion classes) dictates little comprehensive commenting or critical feedback on writing, and instead lends itself to methods of grading that would take the least amount of time possible. Wellesley was not the only school to use this model at this time; it is clear that Wellesley, like Mount Holyoke and so many other institutions of the time, was being influenced by Harvard. The presence of Carpenter and Baker actually indicates that Wellesley may even have been *more* influenced by Harvard than other schools, although again, without a description of actual classroom practices, it is difficult to know whether the Harvard influence was positive or negative. In 1894, for example, an issue of *Outlook* ran a column on Wellesley College. Within the column is a note that "an important advance has been lately made in the department of rhetoric and English composition. The course has been greatly extended, new and stimulating methods have been introduced, and the outcome is a corresponding enthusiasm and improvement on the part of the students" (Guild 99). It seems, then, that students responded positively to the changes being made.

In addition to written work in argumentation, students at Wellesley at this time also had the option of debate. It was, as noted earlier in the 1890 President's Annual Report, a component of Course II in the rhetoric sequence. Known as the course in Argument and Oratory, the fact that "special attention [is] given to debates written and spoken" is an early, overt statement of Wellesley's commitment to train women to speak and debate publicly.

Baker, as Connors shows, was very involved with debating at Harvard, and as such, may have been influential in introducing it to Wellesley as well. Baker's formal title at Harvard at the time was in fact "Argumentative Composition Instructor and Professor." Baker taught the junior and senior level forensics courses at both Radcliffe and Harvard throughout the 1890s (Bordelon, "A Reassessment" 766). In "Intercollegiate Debating," Baker defined debate as "an intellectual sport," one that needed to be developed in order to train students for future participation in political arenas (Bordelon, "A Reassessment" 774). In 1895, he wrote *Principles of Argumentation*, which emphasized the teaching of logic and debate. By 1895, Baker is listed in Wellesley's President's Annual Report as the instructor of record for a course titled Argumentative Composition. The course description lists "a brief based on a masterpiece of argumentative composition" (22). It is not clear whether or not there was an oral component to the course.

Outside of the argumentative composition course, students were also involved in intramural debating. Intramural and intercollegiate debating occurred between the Seven Sisters colleges, indicating that Mr. Baker's presence helped women to practice the argumentation skills they had learned. Wellesley in fact had a debate club as early as the 1880s, as did Mount Holyoke (Conway 215). According to Katherine Conway, Wellesley and Vassar "staged the first women's intercollegiate debate in 1902, before a public audience" (217). Women's suffrage was often the targeted topic for debate and offered women a rallying point and a wider audience than other topics might have.

In addition to Baker, George Carpenter also taught at Wellesley. Less is known about Carpenter at this point, other than analyses of his textbooks (see Kitzhaber or Connors, for example). Stewart and Stewart do note that Carpenter was both a lifelong friend and collaborator with Fred Newton Scott, indicating at least some predilection on his part for progressive thinking. The two men, along with F. T. Baker, collaborated in 1903 on a book called *The Teaching of English* (70). Carpenter, in contrast to George Baker, was initially hired to dovetail the Harvard forensic system with writing that students were doing in other disciplines, in order to create an early Writing Across the Curriculum program. Carpenter seems to have viewed this as an opportunity to get students to think about doing composition work in context with the writing in their own discipline, evidenced by his delight at the opportunities this type of writing instruction would offer: "'What could be better drill in composition than these reports, theses, and the like, prepared for instructors in history, philosophy, or science? The man who thought punctuation a useless and finicky operation finds that he must master it if he wants to make perfectly intelligible what he has to say on metallurgical methods in the mines of Bolivia'" (qtd. in Russell, *Writing in the Academic Disciplines* 108–109). While the "drill in composition" could reflect a current-traditional approach, the idea of having students learn grammar and usage in the context of their own writing is certainly a progressive one. Additionally, it seems unlikely Fred Newton Scott would collaborate with someone who did not share at least some of his own views.

Carpenter left Wellesley in 1893 in order to chair the English department at Columbia. Upon his departure, he recommended Hart as his successor. This seems a somewhat odd move, since Baker was still an instructor there as well. Given the changes the two were able to make, one would surmise that Baker would have taken over the department once Carpenter left, but this was not the case. Baker did not stay long after Carpenter, however, leaving Wellesley in 1895 in order to take a position in Yale's English department; it seems likely he never planned to become a permanent member of the Wellesley faculty. With the exit of both Baker and Carpenter, a new and more openly progressive leader took charge.

The Pedagogy of "Miss Hart"

As the previous chapter indicates, perhaps the most difficult part of recovery work is attempting to recover the various pedagogical and theoretical views of individual instructors. While their jobs are public, their words are most often not recorded, and their actions are documented in ways that do not usually sustain analysis (such as course listings). Like her counterpart Clara Stevens, Sophie Chantal Hart published very little during her lifetime, and only one of the articles she published ("English in the College") was published in a scholarly journal. As a result, much of the interpretive work done on Sophie Chantal Hart must be speculative in nature and involve both critical imagining and strategic contemplation.

Some factual information does exist regarding Hart. It is known, for example, that Sophie Hart was actually originally hired in 1892 to assist Baker and Carpenter, and as a Radcliffe graduate, she knew both men prior to this. Transcripts show that while at Radcliffe, Hart took English 1 (Lectures based on Hill's *Principles of Rhetoric*), English 3 (Forensics, Lectures on Argumentative Composition), and English 6 (The Drama), all taught by Baker (English 1 was co-taught with Professor Briggs). In a 1904 survey, Hart also lists Baker, Carpenter, and Briggs as references for "previous work" (Radcliffe Alumnae Biographical Files). Hart gives some insight into the reorganization of the Wellesley department through a letter written to the Radcliffe *Alumnae Quarterly* in 1942. Hart writes: "After graduation from Radcliffe I went directly to teach at Wellesley College in the Department of Rhetoric and English Composition, chosen by Professor George Pierce Baker and Professor George Carpenter . . . to assist in the reorganization of English work at Wellesley under their leadership" (Radcliffe Alumnae Biographical Files). Clearly, Baker and Carpenter had faith in her teaching and leadership abilities.

After Carpenter's departure, Hart was recommended to head the department. Hart was appointed the chair of the English Composition Department in 1897, and "through her effort delightful, practical, and cultural courses in writing were developed" (Prentiss 182). In 1898, just a year after her appointment as chair, she received her master's degree in Rhetoric from the University of Michigan. Like her contemporary, Clara Stevens, Hart was influenced by her experience in the Michigan department, with its heavy Deweyian progressivist tendencies. Her progressivist methods must have left an impression on the department, simply because of the length of time she spent at Wellesley. Hart taught at Wellesley for an impressive forty-five years and chaired the department for thirty-eight years.

Course offerings typically reflect the skills and interest of current faculty at any institution. Wellesley's course offerings prior to Sophie Chantal Hart (as well as after her arrival) are no exception. In 1895, while the department was still under the leadership of Carpenter and Baker, course offerings included eight courses. A weekly themes course (the Elements and Qualities of Style) was offered, as well as a course in Exposition and Criticism that required themes once every three weeks. Argumentative Composition, Newspaper Work, Daily Themes (a course open only to upperclassmen), and Anglo-Saxon Language and Literature were also offered (President's Annual Report 1895). Baker taught the course in Argumentative Composition. By 1903, however, the department had been under the guidance of Miss Hart for several years, and changes in the course offerings are apparent. The courses Hart added would remain in place, with few changes, until her departure. The overall structure included a General Survey course, required of all freshmen, and Exposition and Criticism, required for a degree (and typically taken by sophomores). Other offerings included Argumentative Composition, Studies in Verse forms, Long and Short Themes, Old English, The Theory and History of Criticism, History of the English Language, Principles of Rhetoric and Composition (a one-hour elective to be taken in addition to the required General Survey course), Debates, and Advanced Course in English Composition (Wellesley College Course Catalog, 1903–04). While the courses in Old English and History of the English Language would become part of the English language department by 1906, the other courses remained, with various titles and numberings, throughout the rest of Hart's tenure. Other courses were added and taken away, but with little frequency. For example, by the 1920s, a course in Journalistic writing was listed, as was one in the Studies of Contemporary Writing (Wellesley College Course Catalog, 1926–27). Short and Long Theme writing, however, remained, as did the Advanced Course in English Composition. Under Hart's direction, then, a stable and coherent experience in rhetoric and composition was provided for the students.

While course catalogs can tell historians what the content of the program was, they cannot comment on particular pedagogies. Hart's methods of teaching were a direct reflection of her graduate training. From all accounts, Hart led the department by progressive example. In "English Composition—An Interpretation," Hart herself lays out her views about the teaching of composition, "a quite special field of interest" (373). Her views are similar to Stevens's, and reflect progressive ideas about individual power and connected experiences. Hart believed the ultimate goal of teaching composition was to

> help an individual possess, really possess, the content of her mind, to correlate ideas, to discover her reactions to ideas and connections between things which have just begun to dawn, enchantingly, on the horizon of the mind. Composition work, seven tenths of it, is evoking in students an awareness of the multiplicity and richness of experience they are living through today; of values in it that they have never isolated before. It is bringing these values into the foreground of consciousness! It is arousing the desire to penetrate these values further, then to weave them into an artistic pattern. (373)

It is clear Hart believed less in writing for writing's sake than for the critical and analytical thinking skills students could work at developing. According to this passage, Hart also believed in the connectedness of experience. Through connected experience, students could begin to see relationships they could then make clear through their writing. Here, perhaps more than anywhere else, the influence of Dewey and Scott on Hart becomes clear. Deweyian notions of connected experience, and the importance of recognizing the connections between a variety of experiences, were carried out in Hart's philosophy. Such work with connected experiences also assumes students are writing about the world around them. In other words, students were not writing abstract themes on topics entirely unfamiliar to them, but were instead working with the material they would have been most familiar with—that of their own experience. In answer to the question of how much undergraduates could possibly use experience as a vehicle for writing, Hart notes that "they have everything they have ever seen, countryside, home, relatives, family attitudes, the sense of life prevailing about them, and a veritable Niagra of ideas pouring in from every direction upon them" (373). Hart reinforced the notion of carefully analyzing experience and then relating it to other experiences. She also clearly values students as knowers, and hopes to help them express the "multiplicity of richness" of their experiences in writing (373). The fact that Hart felt that "seven tenths" of composition work was comprised of this indicates that any predisposition she had toward teaching grammar or usage was relegated to the remaining three-tenths of her equation. Carefully constructed content based on knowledge, therefore, was the focus of Hart's pedagogy.

Hart's emphasis on students' making their own meaning and forming their own thoughts out of their own experiences is part of what Cy Knoblauch and Lil Brannon label modern rhetoric, which emphasizes students making meaning: "Making meaning is regarded as a competence, with clarity and correctness among the more mature manifestations of that competence" (103). This philosophy is also in keeping with Fred Newton Scott's idea that writing was much like building a house; the writer must have the ability to make the house structurally sound, but if there were a few small flaws, the house would not fall. In the same vein, Hart is here advocating that the primary instruction in writing should focus on the ability to build the frame for that house, with attention to adornment later. Such a view allows teachers to encourage students to write (in much the way Hart seems to have) because it values what they have to say, even if the way they choose to say it is seen as technically and grammatically flawed. As Knoblauch and Brannon point out, a writer's maturity will continue to develop "in any circumstances where the writer is motivated to seek improved facility because his or her meanings, and efforts to make meaning, are valued by readers and therefore personally valuable as well" (103). As the previous passage indicates, Hart's interest in her students' experience shows she indeed did value them, and in encouraging them to make meaning from those experiences, she was working from a Deweyian progressivist model.

It is also possible to extrapolate about Hart's methods from existing exams. Wellesley's archives has a rich collection of exams from rhetoric classes. While these exams cannot tell us what a particular class actually looked like, changes in focus in the department can be seen through the exams. In 1893, for example, just one year after Hart's arrival, a mid-year exam for English Composition I reflects a focus on correctness. The exam contains some seventeen sentences for students to properly punctuate and asks students to define different types of sentences. In addition, they are asked to correctly choose words such as *will* versus *should* and *would* versus *should* for a series of sentences. Students are also asked to locate the faults in a paragraph. The only questions which rise above superficial matters of correctness are the last two:

1. What advice about paragraphs would you give to an inexperienced friend who was about to write an essay?
2. Distinguish Force from Clearness? How far is it dependent on Clearness? What devices for securing Force do you suggest? What quality, or qualities, should you like your writing to possess? Why? (Wellesley College, English Department Papers)

Overall, the exam is limited in scope, and as previously stated, cannot provide information about pedagogical methods. However, it reflects an overall focus on correctness rather than sustained critique. Even the two questions that center on the work of the student are aimed at correct answers.

An exam from English Composition I in 1901, nine years after Hart's arrival, has a more progressive tone and is similar to exams students recalled from Fred Newton Scott's class at Michigan. It begins with "what are the three principles of composition? Tell fully what each principle demands." It also covers the purpose and structure of the paragraph, and asks students to "name four devices for securing paragraph coherence, and illustrate their use in a brief paragraph." The exam not only asks students to know the rules of writing but also to be able to use them. Later exams ask students to describe methods for achieving coherence and unity in essay writing.

In a throwback to the earlier exam, the 1901 exam does ask for definitions. For example, students are asked to define the difference between a periodic and balanced sentence. However, students are then asked to discuss the differences, as well as the advantages and disadvantages of using each. In this way, students are asked to provide information about and reflection on their decisions.

A 1905 exam for English I at Wellesley is remarkably similar to a student recollection of one of Fred Newton Scott's exams. Five lengthy sentences are offered in the Wellesley exam, and the instructions are to "rewrite the following sentences. In each case, give clear, definite reasons for your revision." A student from Fred Newton Scott's Usage and Diction class recalled a similar exam. James Corcoran recalled the final exam question,

> which was about as follows: 'Describe the day, and in doing so use one of the following words: gray, dark, dreary, cold, melancholy, somber'—and about a million other synonyms that I no longer remember. Then came a sub-question, (b),

> which nearly floored us. It read: 'Give your reason for selecting the adjective that you use, and tell how it differs in meaning from each of the other adjectives'—although you probably said 'every one' instead of 'each.' (Corcoran)

Both assignments ask the writers to critically reflect on the choices they make. The questions do not involve mere skill drills, but tests of a student's ability to both acquire and use certain types of knowledge and to defend the decisions they make.

While curriculum design and final exams can offer programmatic insights, perhaps the most direct and telling statement regarding Hart's pedagogy is found in a tribute written to her on her retirement in 1937. Dorothy Havens Chappell, Class of 1914, composed a letter to the *Wellesley Magazine,* in which she repeatedly refers to Miss Hart not as a teacher, but as a "teacher-listener," who continually expected her students to have something to contribute verbally to class. Chappell goes on to describe Hart's teaching in the following way:

> It is typical of her as a skilled lecturer that she lectured little in class. By the magic of her true teaching, she built up thoughts in the students, and drew from them those very soundings of truth. Sitting at a lecture of hers one feels participation and activity. After a lecture she looks calm and her audience looks exercised and eager. She, with that air of listening rather than speaking, does not overstress what is already grasped, but lightly goes on to new fabrication of ideas resting on the foundation so strongly cemented by sincerity of attention and mutual thought. (12)

Such a description parallels modern composition's denigration of learning-by-lecture, and also shows Hart's move to much more progressive methods than the divided lecture/discussion sections originally used. Such teaching methods also compare to the descriptions of Clara Stevens's teaching, and both involve Shor's modern notions of the critical classroom, where the teacher uses thought-provoking critical conversation as a tool for learning and for creating a liberatory culture. They also invoke current descriptions of the goals for feminist pedagogy. Walker, Geertsema, and Barnett view participatory learning and the development of voice as key components of feminist pedagogy. According to them, in a feminist classroom, "the teacher surrenders her position as an authority who transmits information to empty vessels" (185). In addition, feminist pedagogy helps students make connections, particularly between their lives and their class work (185). Both of these features are clear in Hart's pedagogy. Hart's reality was not one of the expert lecturer, but instead involved a committed teacher-learner. This notion was seconded by former student Virginia Westervelt, Class of 1935, who remembered that Hart warned "that students should not become too dependent on the guidance and inspiration of a teacher; the interest should be in ideas, not in a person; and a teacher's joy should be in subject matter, in principle, rather than information" (Chappell 183). Hart's methods, rather than involving the passive transmission of knowledge from teacher to student, instead involved active dialogue between the teacher and the student, with both learning from each other and both drawing on their own experiences to create connections, and therefore new knowledge.

Hart's one scholarly piece of work, published in 1902, also gives an overview of her pedagogical interests. "English in the College," published in *The School Review* in 1902, was the result of a research project Hart apparently undertook to gather information about the status of composition in various colleges. To this end, Hart includes the following survey as part of her article, and this survey indicates the kinds of questions she thought were important in developing curriculum:

1. How many hours of required work are there in English composition and rhetoric as distinguished from literature?
2. How many hours of elective work?
3. How often do you have written work, (*a*) prepared outside class, (*b*) done in class?
4. To what extent are theme subjects taken (*a*) from the literature studied? (*b*) from the student's daily life, observation, and experience? (*c*) from work done in other departments of the college exclusive of the English department?
5. How much time is given to the reading of themes in class? Is the reading done by the instructor or the student?
6. Are the themes written with reference to a specific audience suggested by the instructor or chosen by the student?
7. In the early work of the course is facility or correctness made the immediate aim?
8. To what extent is the entire rewriting of themes required?

9. What amount of time per month is given by the instructor to personal conference with individual students on the written work?
10. Have you courses in which the problems of English composition are considered with reference to training students who intend to teach English in the secondary schools?
11. Along what lines do you see most need of improvement in the English teaching of your college?
12. What recommendations have you to send back to teachers of English in the preparatory schools fitting for your college? (364)

While the origins of this survey are unclear, one can reasonably assume Hart herself created it since she includes it along with the results in her article. Hart's survey interestingly echoes many of modern composition's concerns: what is the role of revision in writing instruction? What (if any) link is there between the work in the composition department and the work in other departments of the college? What is (and what should be) the link between literature and composition? What value should be placed on revision, and how is it defined? How much connection is the student able to make between life experience and writing? Such issues are implicitly addressed in Hart's questions. Some possible responses are implicitly addressed in the answers she reports.

Hart notes that of the schools surveyed (there were at least ten), most indicate that a third to a half of classroom time is spent discussing themes. Hart feels this is not enough; more time spent on discussing theme work will help students to make the connection between the theoretical work of the course and the actual practical implications of it: "Our composition teaching, as I said a moment ago, is suffering from too much theory, from too little practical application to the matter at hand. No instructor can ever be sure that his students are not bandying about mere terms and empty names until they are put to the test of criticising [sic] themes" (369). Workshopping writing is clearly privileged here, and Hart's notions of connected teaching are also apparent. Fred Newton Scott and Gertrude Buck also advocated such learning strategies as part of their commitment to Deweyian pedagogy in writing instruction.

Hart also makes it clear elsewhere in the article that she believes the teaching of rhetoric (here defined as theoretical in nature) must be connected with the actual act of composing, reflecting Scott's (and Dewey's) belief in connected learning. In addition to her comments regarding theory and application, Hart also criticizes the system in place for a failure to utilize Deweyian progressive theories of teaching. While Hart does not say so explicitly, a major facet of Deweyian progressivism asked students to learn through action rather than through theory. Hart notes that

> the emphasis at present falls in such a way as to lead one to suppose that we solemnly teach rhetoric as an end in itself rather than as means to composition. In painting and drawing, it is acknowledged that the student learns by *doing*; in English composition, it seems to be supposed that the student learns by copious advice as to how to do. (369)

Hart's connection here indicates her own inclination toward students learning to write by *writing*, a point modern compositionists have continually reinforced as well.

Hart also indicates a predisposition toward revision when she reveals that responses submitted from "several of the leading colleges" report that sixty to seventy-five percent of the themes written in the colleges were subject to revision. These results do not reveal the types of themes that were written, or whether they were short or long, factors Hart seems to indicate make a difference in the decision to revise. As well, there is little indication as to what form that revision work might have taken. It is possible, of course, that many of the schools defined revision as little more than having students alter errors the instructor found for them. In any case, Hart prioritizes long themes as primarily needing revision, and seems dismayed that a larger percentage of time is not spent on theme revision. Hart also incorporates the belief that discussion of the themes will help students toward revising them, invoking an early workshop model. Hart notes, "the discussion of themes in class, if wisely conducted, will throw new points of view on the matter as well as the form; will enable the student to re-envisage his material, will send him away eager to reconstitute it in the larger, more pregnant relations which the discussion has revealed" (370). Such a pedagogical belief would have also had much greater benefit to Hart as a writing teacher; student papers that have already been subject to revision would have been less time-consuming to grade. In addition, such comments show that Hart was advocating workshopping of papers in her classroom, if students were actively discussing the themes in class with revision as the ultimate goal.

In her text, Hart includes several excerpts from responses to the survey, submitted by six different faculty members at six different institutions, each answering the question of what recommendations professors had for preparatory school teachers. Hart includes one short excerpt from "Professor Ganung [*sic*] of Amherst." Hart quotes Genung as stating that in order to improve the state of composition instruction, "there ought to be more drill in simple English grammar, and a more vital, less exclusively mechanical, approach to the work of composition" (374). Genung's response creates an interesting juxtaposition here, on the one hand advocating a seemingly progressive goal of a less mechanical approach to teaching, but in the same breath proposing more of the skill-drills that the more scientific and current-traditional approach advocated. More in keeping with Hart's own pedagogy was a response from a Professor Hart of Cornell, who advocated teaching better thinking as the primary tool for better writing. "Our Cornell experience is that the most difficult thing to overcome is the lack of thought. Many of our freshmen seem to believe that anything patched up in grammatical shape will pass for writing" (373). Hart does not add any of her own commentary to those responses and there is little indication of any level of agreement or disagreement on her part.

Overall, Hart's survey offers an interesting tool for thinking about her work and comparing it to the work of others. Hart ends her article by concluding that the best way of continuing to improve writing standards is to continue to advocate increased progressive activity at the elementary and secondary level. Hart lauds the schools for their "splendid work in sending up students increasingly well trained" (373), which is no small compliment from an instructor at a school that originally established its own secondary level schools for that very purpose. Hart's very notion of the continued improvement of education is by nature part of the educational Progressive Movement.

One question Hart does not raise in her survey is that of ideal class sizes and workload. Workload issues at a variety of institutions continued to plague progress toward more individualized instruction, and composition courses at Wellesley were no exception. While earlier records noted that Hart taught approximately two hundred students while Professors Baker and Carpenter were affiliated with the department, there is no indication that these numbers decreased, and in fact, for Hart, they increased throughout her tenure at Wellesley. Early records show incremental leaps in the numbers of students taking courses in the composition department. The President's Annual Report from 1909 shows a total of 319 students in the required freshman course (then called The Elements and Qualities of Style), although there were multiple instructors. By 1912 that had jumped to 417 and the numbers at the college continued to rise. Dealey's research on the popularity of different subjects studied at women's colleges shows that 82% of Wellesley students in 1915 took 10% or more of their work in the English department, reflecting not only the fact that students were required to take courses in English but also that they chose English electives at a high rate (355).

In addition to a shortage of instructors, physical facilities at Wellesley were also at a premium and did not keep up with the increased enrollment. It is possible to critically imagine the work that went on in the department's individual conferences through descriptions of their physical space. Much like the University of Michigan's Department of Rhetoric, the Wellesley faculty, too, could not conference individually with students in any kind of private setting. In fact, the President's Annual Report of 1908–09, in recommending building more academic buildings, noted that "the English Composition and English Literature departments are in much the same condition [as the sciences]—one small office where all business interviews between a large corps of teachers and their students must be conducted with the result of embarrassment and loss of efficiency" (15). The next year's report laments similar conditions, commenting that

> there are very few office rooms which can be used for consultation. A large part of the effectiveness of the work in English depends upon individual criticism from the instructor. This year there have been ten instructors in the department of English Composition holding office hours in ends of corridors and in corners of rooms where there was nothing like proper privacy, so that neither the instructor nor the student could feel at ease. (7)

Certainly individual conferences would have been difficult at best under such circumstances.

While the department did eventually secure better quarters, including its own reading room in the new library (seating thirty-six), the overall teaching conditions and high student loads did not improve. Hart in fact resigned the position of Chair of the English Department in 1935, noting she was not doing so because of failing health (as had apparently been rumored), but because she had a heavier teaching load than anyone else in the department. The personal letter indicates that she is working at full capacity, the Drama course having over one hundred students, History of Criticism with seventy, and Advanced Composition "full to the limit," although it is not entirely clear what this means (Personal Papers). In any case, it seems Hart still had at least two hundred students, an unreasonable number by any standard for effective college level instruction in writing. To maintain the responsibilities of chair as well seems either superhuman or insane. Such a workload, heavier than anyone else's, more than indicates Hart's dedication to her teaching.

Hart's workload, however, does not seem to be atypical for women's college professors of the time period. Jo Ann Campbell, in "Women's Work, Worthy Work: Composition Instruction at Vassar College, 1897–1922," notes the same types of workloads among instructors there. Laura Johnson Wylie, Professor of English at Vassar, worked to collect data about teaching loads. During Wylie's first year at Vassar (1894), she was responsible for two classes in argumentation, with sixty students each, and four sections of freshmen with forty-five each. This total load of three hundred students, as Wylie was well aware, was an impediment to good teaching. Wylie noted that, comparatively, other departments had much lighter teaching loads. "The number of students per teacher in English was 148.7; it was 39.4 in zoology and 100.5 in Greek" (Campbell 31). The comparable conditions at Vassar may have made it even more difficult for instructors such as Hart to negotiate lighter course loads. It is obvious by the number of students Hart was teaching in 1935 (over two hundred) that such progress was still extremely slow to manifest itself. It is also clear from such a load that teaching at Wellesley (and at Vassar) was the ultimate priority, which may at least partially explain Hart's limited publishing career. Imagining teaching such numbers gives modern readers a sense of the physical conditions under which teachers like Hart worked.

Sophie Chantal Hart, as well as participating in progressive teaching practices, was also an advocate for student and faculty participation in service areas that had become popular during the Progressive Era. Wellesley College's faculty expressed an overall belief in the value of service. Vida Scudder, for example, advocated for a college student to develop an understanding that all women could be both "of superior intellect [and] moral force" (Palmieri, "Symmetrical Womanhood" 20). Hart, like her colleagues, saw education as not only a way of curing social ills but also as a way of recruiting new women to public service. Hart stated that Wellesley's students should be "sucked into this new vortex of college thought, which discloses [. . .] the conduct of life in accordance with the ideals of service" (Palmieri, "Symmetrical Womanhood" 20). It is clear, then, that Hart participated in Progressive Era views in ways other than those evidenced in her pedagogy.

Role modeling would have helped students see the benefits and rewards of active participation. Many Progressive Era professors, including those at Wellesley and Mount Holyoke, were themselves active in political and social reform movements, and encouraged their students to become engaged in such work as well. While many women continued to be frustrated by the receptions they received, they still continued to try to participate and to try to remain active in learning about and participating in society at large. Hart, for example, encouraged students to write about suffrage, going so far as to modify the content of a Harvard lesson book in order to be more appealing to female students. Among her modifications were the additions of six suffrage topics (Conway 214). Hart also noted in "The Relation of College Experience" that "college experience offers other and very practical agencies which train for later social needs, and which lead to the same goal of social consciousness" (57). In particular, Hart was referring to the students' participation in student government, which she felt was training for future *active* participation in the citizenship at large. Nowhere does she mention that these women might have been silenced in their efforts to speak outside of the college; she simply assumes a place for their voices. This is in keeping with a type of discourse Berlin identifies as Fred Newton Scott's "democratic rhetoric of public discourse" (*Rhetoric and Reality* 50). Through such a progressive approach, Hart encouraged a student to see herself as part of a larger social context, combine her knowledge and her experience with language, and constantly evaluate her own perspectives in light of her audience and community at large. Likewise, Hart, in "English Composition—An Interpretation," notes that teaching composition requires "a profound faith in the cultural value of so assimilating and so gaining power to express what one knows as to make it intimately, vitally, one's very own" (373). Thus, Hart, like Stevens, viewed training in written and oral discourse as a way for students to gain agency and voice—and thereby power. This power could in turn be used publicly.

In addition to her advocacy in social reform issues, Hart also believed in cultural education rather than assimilation. While administrative progressivism wanted to create a uniform American culture, Hart evidences a concern that her students should understand, rather than assimilate, difference. It seems somewhat ironic that she would pursue this idea at a largely homogenous place like Wellesley. While there were a few minority students, a few non-Protestants and a few students on scholarship, the large majority were white, Protestant and upper-middle class. There were, however, differences in ethnic origins and some international students. It is clear that Hart, at least, tried to address some of these differences and help other students gain an understanding of those differences when she organized students of different nationalities to "investigate" internationalism (Palmieri, *In Adamless Eden* 246). While it is unclear whether or not students wrote about these investigations, Hart made clear attempts at having her students understand and respect difference.

Hart, like Stevens, also seemed to have a complex understanding of the role of teacher. She was known for socializing with her students, and thus developing closer relationships with them than the traditional teacher/student dichotomy would allow. One student's recollection of her, for example, includes the following reminiscence about Halloween: "It is too funny to see how sociable faculty are with the students. Miss Hart, our English instructor, was meandering about in the crowd, in full ghost costume like any of us [. . .]" (Manwaring in Palmieri 188). Like Clara Stevens, Hart interacted with her students in a variety of settings, not limited to the classroom.

Sophie Chantal Hart retired from the Wellesley English department in 1937, after forty-five years as an instructor and thirty-eight years as chair of the department. Throughout her tenure, she continued to implement and teach a variety of courses in rhetorical theory. She continued to advocate for progressive methods of instruction and to combat the idea that writing instruction was meant to be in service to other disciplines. After Hart's retirement, however, the Department of Composition began to slowly fold. Rather than distinct courses in Argumentation, Narrative, and Exposition, the whole of writing instruction began to slowly move towards a single required freshman course, with upper level courses increasingly becoming elective. In 1937, a single Department of English was proposed (perhaps coincidentally the year Hart retired), although no further attempts toward amalgamation were made until 1945. Complete amalgamation of the two departments took place in 1947, and writing instruction was continually phased out from that point on. Patrick Quinn, the new chair of the department, noted in a letter in 1959 that "with the retirement of Miss Prentiss this year we lose the one person in the department whose interest was emphatically if not exclusively in the composition course. It is likely that the department can now be characterized as a literature department" (Letter to President Clapp). As a result of Miss Prentiss's retirement, the last few courses offered that involved writing sequence work were disbanded as Wellesley too underwent changes typical of the times.

The progress of writing instruction at Wellesley parallels that of comparable schools such as Mount Holyoke. Mount Holyoke went from progressive methods to current-traditional ones and back to progressive methods under the leadership of Clara Stevens. Perhaps because it was founded so much later, and so much closer to the Progressive Era, Wellesley seems to only have experienced a brief burst of the current-traditionalism in writing and English studies that its sister school had. Little to nothing is known about the earliest instruction at Wellesley, up until the point where George Baker and George Carpenter entered the scene, and when Sophie Hart took over the department. While ultimately it is impossible to know what effect her graduate work at Michigan had on her teaching, it is possible to critically imagine that it solidified and furthered the development of her views of progressive teaching. Regardless, Hart's influence on her students was extensive. She was a vital member of her department, and it is clear that her strong individual presence kept the department in existence. Indeed, within only twenty years after her departure, writing studies at Wellesley had been phased out and superceded by literature.

In conclusion, Deweyian progressivism had a much wider impact on college writing departments than is often recognized. One such impact was at the level of the women's college, and it more specifically manifested itself in the writing instruction delivered there. Sophie Chantal Hart's role as the chair of Wellesley's English department, and more importantly as a progressive role model for other instructors, has historically been overlooked. Moreover, Hart's story contributes to the list of progressive pedagogues, making it clear she and women like her were not anomalies. Like Clara Stevens at Mount Holyoke, like Laura Johnson Wylie and Gertrude Buck at Vassar, and like countless other pedagogues of her time, Hart was a product of a progressive education that seems to have had little overall influence but rather a large impact in a small circle. When viewed in conjunction with the historical work of other women and progressive pedagogues, the history Stevens and Hart provide allows today's composition scholars to see that progressive pedagogy has had an integral presence in the history of composition. Stevens's and Hart's contributions are marked by views of students as knowers and attempts at student empowerment through writing. Reclamation of these two scholar-pedagogues, then, is important in developing a historical timeline of progressive pedagogy and its effects on writing instruction and women's education.

5 Learning from the Past, Looking to the Future

> *History is about telling stories. [. . .] History is better defined as an ongoing tension between stories that have been told and stories that might be told. In this sense, it is more useful to think of history as an ethical and political practice than as an epistemology with a clear ontological status.*
>
> —Lynn Hunt

> *How shall the young become acquainted with the past in such a way that the acquaintance is a potent agent in appreciation of the living present?*
>
> —John Dewey

Rethinking the history of composition using a feminist lens of critical imagining allows for an expanded view of our past, a way to render our current configurations meaningful and to offer a sense that there is a viable future for composition studies. Slowly and carefully reading the past and engaging the evidence in a dialogue adds specifics to our general knowledge. It also helps reinscribe and reinterpret our stories of the past. As Frederick Nietzsche said, "the more different eyes we can put on in order to view a given spectacle, the more complete will be our conception of it, the greater our 'objectivity'" (291). While that picture (and that objectivity) can never be pure or whole, ethical research practices require that we at least try to render it as complete as possible. As David Gold reminds us about his own retelling of Progressive Era pedagogies, "these stories are necessarily incomplete. But they are necessary" (152). In part, this means looking at unknown and unexplored sources, including those that address women's issues and feminist practices. According to Kirsch and Royster, "excellence [in historical research] also means recognizing what was made possible for us as feminist rhetorical scholars through other women's work, how their efforts have enabled us to stand where we are today, and how their visions make it possible for us to see a future, a future worth working for" (664). It also means keeping in mind that there is a value to doing this kind of work, and that it does not necessarily reside in the creation or testing of a new theoretical framework but rather in adding to existing layers of history to create Nietzsche's "objectivity." As Rynbrant reminds us, successful research on historical topics "is an attempt to add to the expanding sociohistorical discourse, which, in part, uncovers the silences of the past" (14). Uncovering historical patterns such as the social connections between Dewey, Scott, Scott's students, and their writing students helps us hear and see the patterns of Progressive Era writing instruction. It makes it possible for us to critically imagine Progressive Era rhetorical practices.

THE CONTINUED NEED FOR RECOVERY

In many ways, current composition theory and Progressive Era pedagogy have much to say to one another, but even though clear connections exist between Progressive Era pedagogues and current theories, one question has continued to perplex me as I worked on this project. Why must we continue to engage in the rewriting of this history? Why are the names of these women not common knowledge, even at their own institutions? Why did the reign of such powerful, charismatic, and enduring teachers end? Where was the next generation to step into their shoes, to fight for their programs, and to continue their legacy? Why did Progressive Era pedagogy seem to be all but dead by 1920 (and definitely by the 1940s), not to be revived until the 1970s?

It is tempting to dismiss some of what happened as circumstantial. Personality clashes, for example, seem to have plagued Sophie Chantal Hart's career and may have contributed to a general disdain for composition at Wellesley. Despite many positive student recollections, Hart had what is known in polite company as a strong personality. Palmieri documents a life-long rivalry between Hart and fellow composition instructor Laura Lockwood. Lockwood noted that Hart "tried to get people to work for her as much as possible" (Palmieri, *In Adamless Eden* 128). Palmieri also describes Hart in her role on the Wellesley Academic Council as "aggressive," "verbally adept," and one of several "warring giants" (129). Hart also had a documented altercation with Helen Drusilla Lockwood, who worked as an instructor at Wellesley for a brief time. Lockwood's files at Vassar College contain a transcription she made of a contentious conversation with Hart. The experience obviously affected her enough that she kept the transcript in her Wellesley files long after she had worked there. Lockwood left for a position at Vassar shortly after the argument, writing in an application letter (for a position at Barnard) that she was "fed up with Wellesley and its hostilities between the Composition and Literature departments" (Palmieri 249). While the two departments functioned well with each other as a whole, it seems that individual personalities within each and between each often did not mix well (perhaps going back to the days of Katherine Lee Bates and her terse comments about composition in 1894). Regardless of conflicts of personality, though, Hart still maintained a well-run, progressive department that served its students well, but was nevertheless collapsed upon her departure.

While Stevens did not share Hart's reputation, her department met with the same fate. Stevens's influence seems to have faded quickly after her departure. As noted in chapter three, while they tried, her peers could not resist the pressures of Roswell Ham to unite the two departments. Perhaps if he had not been president as well as literature faculty, they would have been more successful in their efforts. Perhaps if Stevens had not retired when she did, she might have been able to stave off the collapse of her rhetoric department for longer. This does not explain, though, why there was no strong leader to take over in her absence.

Hart and Stevens's fates were not, unfortunately, unique. However, there seem to be no carefully documented reasons for them. One plausible reason for such a decline in women's roles in rhetoric after 1920 is that it parallels the general decline of progressivism in the United States. With the Great Depression, a World War, continued pressure on women to marry, and the decline of an organized feminist movement, women's numbers began to decrease both as college students and as college professors.[1] These events, particularly World War I, all undermined the rhetoric of social bonds used by progressives in favor of more individualized beliefs (Rodgers 124; Decker 18). In addition, as Gordon observes, "as the reform imperative and women's culture waned, so did women's opportunities to affect public and professional life" (196). Opportunities previously available to women diminished, while those that remained available (including teaching) came without adequate compensation or autonomy. As conservative backlash affected other movements, it also affected progressivism and feminism, and in turn, teaching. Largely citing economic reasons, administrative progressives finally won their arguments for consolidation of departments and devaluation of Deweyian methods. They were too labor intensive and too costly. As well, such methods were too group and community oriented at a time when the focus was shifting to the individual, even within the feminist movement (Gordon 199).

Other factors clearly worked against the sustained success of the progressives. For example, standardized testing, as discussed earlier, had become popular during the early Progressive Era. Its use was increased exponentially, though, by the advent of machine-scored testing. This had a direct affect on writing as well. While the majority of the influence of the Progressive Movement was over by 1920, Russell asserts that by the 1940s, "with machine-scored tests providing the most important measures of performance, essay writing became increasingly distant from the activities of education that mattered most to the system. The 1940s and 1950s saw few studies of essay examinations in the United States" (*Writing in the Academic Disciplines* 241). The new machine technology directly supported the increasing influence of administrative progressivism, and as such, undermined the work of the few progressive teachers left.

In addition to the increase in technology-driven standardized testing, continued departmentalization and a move toward learning discrete information in different areas also contributed to the downfall of Deweyian notions of connected learning by solidifying the role of distinct disciplines and forcing students to study and write within those disciplines only. Students were not seen as individuals studying varying but related information, but instead were subjected to an increasingly uniform curriculum, organized using the new large-scale, industrial and bureaucratic models business had adopted for itself (Edson 64). This affected writing in many ways, including isolating it to a single *service* function that was not seen as scholarly. Russell, in *Writing in the Academic Disciplines*, explores the effects of this change at Columbia around 1920, observing that they even dropped a semester of the required writing course in order to make room for a new required contemporary civilization course (231). This move mirrored such changes at other institutions, and reflected an altered view of the purpose of required writing. It also reflected a change in the amount of required writing. Because the new civilization course "aimed to refine understanding and judgment, not to teach content or disciplinary method [. . .] these less concrete goals, the instructors found, could be accomplished with oral instruction. Instructors were not required to assign papers" (231). Whereas writing had often been an integral part of Progressive Era learning, by the end of the era, it had little to no place. Papers were typically assigned only to sections of high-scoring students who placed into them. Russell tersely comments on the overall effects of this design: "Once again writing became a way of discriminating among students instead of a way of making education general" (231). Writing's place in the academy had thus shifted again as the century progressed.

Writing instruction at this time also moved back toward a focus on the individual within his or her own national sphere. As Berlin notes in *Rhetoric and Reality*, after World War I big business was now defining what progressivism meant, and the focus at this time was on individualism, but a model that ultimately served "middle-class political concerns" (59). For writing, this often meant a focus on the individual that privileged creative forms of writing. The individual, however, was not seen as autonomous. Unlike Deweyian progressivism, new forms of educational theory reinforced an individual within a nationalist and patriotic sphere (Crowley 98). Herbert Croly's 1909 essay "Individual vs. Collective Education" is reflective of this drive, emphasizing that

> national education in its deeper aspect does not differ from individual education. Its efficiency ultimately depends upon the ability of the national consciousness to draw illuminating inferences from the course of the national experience; and its power to draw such inferences must depend upon the persistent and disinterested sincerity with which the attempt is made to realize the national purpose—the democratic ideal of individual and social improvement. (252)

Croly's description makes the assimilation of individual and national interest very clear, even by 1909. Such a view would continue to develop as national concerns (particularly World War I) increased.

Bowles and Gintis, in *Schooling in Capitalist America*, see the largest failure of the Progressive Movement as a failure to critique the economic systems that were developing concurrently with educational ones. Instead, they argue, the Progressive Movement was morality-based, and as such could not sustain itself without a thorough critique of the newly developing "corporate order" (200). Instead,

> Lacking any strong grass-roots support, and self-consciously eschewing any systematic critique of the evolving economic order, it is not surprising that the idealistic Progressives worked in vain for a humanitarian and egalitarian education. More in tune with immediate economic realities, the bureaucratization, tracking, and test-orientation of the school system proceeded smoothly, promoted by seed money from large private foundations, articulated by social scientists at prestigious schools of education, and enthusiastically implemented by business-controlled local school boards. (200)

While elementary and secondary schools were primarily affected by this, so too were colleges and universities, which began to adopt a business mentality that has stayed with them ever since. The consolidation of departments of rhetoric in many places with departments of English directly exemplified this mentality. There was no longer a solid understanding of what a department of rhetoric *did* that would differentiate it or give it cause for a separate existence from an English department.

Lastly, one other factor directly affected the downfall of the progressive women who taught at the institutions I have discussed. Initially, I was puzzled by what seemed like a failure of other women to take over when people like Buck and Scott died, and when Stevens and Hart retired. What makes the collapse of their departments all the more curious is that there were plenty of women who had progressive training and could have stepped into the shoes of women like Hart and Stevens. Gertrude Buck ran a veritable underground railroad trying to persuade students to pursue graduate studies at the University of Michigan, and she was by all accounts quite successful. University of Michigan graduates in rhetoric were in fact partly comprised of women from colleges such as Vassar, Mount Holyoke, Smith, and Wellesley, and many women who were on faculty at those colleges were Michigan graduates. The women's colleges needed trained female faculty and the female faculty needed jobs. Female faculty had often recommended promising students to graduate programs, with the idea of later hiring them back. Rossiter's protégé chains were strong, but only as long as there was graduate work available for those working in rhetorical studies.

Even after Buck's death in 1921, and Hart and Stevens's retirements, numbers indicate that there should have been enough remaining women who were trained in progressive pedagogy to keep these programs alive. It took me a long time to finally realize that the death of Scott and his program sealed the fate of these women. While many women themselves were able to complete master's and doctoral level work, they were not able to teach at research universities. As a result, they did not create their own graduate programs to train future students. Even though they were able to send their own students to Scott's program, eventually that too came to an end. Because Scott had not planned for and trained a successor, because women still weren't able to secure positions as university faculty in any numbers (Clifford xi), and because the Progressive Era was coming to a close when Scott retired, there was no place left where students could receive graduate degrees in rhetoric and thus carry on the progressive work Dewey had begun and Scott had co-opted for rhetoric and composition. Protégé chains were no longer sustainable.

The fact that these women were still not particularly welcome at doctoral level institutions by the end of the Progressive Era is indicative of larger problems within the Progressive Era itself. As Robyn Muncy comments in "The Ambiguous Legacies of Women's Progressivism," one the ironies of Progressive Era social reform carried out by middle and upper class women was that they often did not gain any economic rights for themselves. While they were able to take on previously unheld roles in the public sector, they were unofficial. While they were able to negotiate labor reform for working class women, they also reinforced the notion of women as weak. "This image of working women, while justifying legislation that genuinely helped many, made it impossible for women to compete effectively with men in many sectors of the labor market" (16). By the end of the Progressive Era, this had also affected teaching and other professions typically occupied by women. While female teachers were still accepted at lower levels, collegiate and in particular university level positions were still reserved for men. Geraldine Clifford makes this clear in her introduction to *Lone Voyagers: Academic Women in Coeducational Institutions, 1870–1937* when she comments that women never found a critical mass as professors at large coeducational institutions the way they had at women's colleges. Even those who did gain employment at universities usually did so as teaching assistants or non-tenured assistant professors, if they could get jobs there at all. "Moreover, most women faculty in the United States were confined to lower-status institutions: in normal schools and their successor institutions, the state teachers' colleges; junior and community colleges; public colleges and universities of lesser rank; and little-known church-sponsored colleges" (xi). This left them in no position to train new faculty members to take their places or to develop powerful new programs in composition and rhetoric. As noted earlier, such reinscription of the domestic views of women can be seen even in Dewey's limited visions of women's roles.

Scott, too, did not see a place for female teachers at the university, at least not at the University of Michigan. While he clearly supported the female students who worked with him, an incident recorded in his daybook in 1921 makes his ambiguous feelings about women at Michigan clear. According to Stewart and Stewart, in 1921 a woman appeared in his office looking for work as an instructor, "but 'he [Dean Effinger] agreed with me that a women instructor [sic] was undesirable at present.' In general, women faculty were to be found primarily in the women's colleges like Vassar or Mount Holyoke, or in small private schools" (172). Scott's reaction seems very curious, especially as late as 1921, but no further documentation seems to exist that might clarify his comments. In any case, he makes it clear that even at a progressive institution, women's places were still circumscribed.

All of these convergent factors worked to destroy what had been, ultimately, a life's work for women like Hart and Stevens. Their work in many ways was circumstantial and highly contextual; they could not have achieved what they did had they been born either fifty years earlier or later. It has now become the job of modern historians to recover their work, gain wisdom from it, and hope we can avoid a similar aftermath. We must also hope the growing body of scholarship about women's lives does not cycle out of favor yet again, leaving our own work to be later rediscovered. This is particularly vital, because, as Rynbrandt points out, "there is a tendency to dismiss these women and devalue their contributions to women and society. There is a danger that we may have discovered these lost women in the past only to lose them again by contemporary judgments which render them irrelevant at best, and dangerous at worst" (xii). Dismissing these histories, though, leaves a continually fragmented history of composition and rhetorical studies that needs constant reimagining and reconstruction.

As a historian, I have learned much from investigating Stevens and Hart and linking their work to the Progressive Era and the programs that provided their training. While scholars such as Berlin and Connors have worked on this time period, it is clear to me that their early work, while important, has simply not been complex enough. These histories are much richer and more complicated than historians (myself included) have ever thought. We need to look at the way the different threads could be brought together in order to create more complex pictures. The Progressive Era's effects on writing instruction as a whole merit more exploration, and certainly the work of the Deweyian scholars, pedagogues, and writing program administrators within it have much to teach us.

It also has become clear to me through my research that academic programs are never really stable. They follow the ebbs and tides of educational, social, and political events and movements. We need to remember that our own departments and programs are not as stable as we like to think. The downfall of Scott's program was not the anomalous event that has been portrayed in history; in fact, it was part of a larger collapse of programs in many institutions. We need to let this serve as a warning to us as compositionists, that programs can be wholly dependent on individuals and localized events, without which they cannot continue. Unlike Scott and Hart and Stevens, we must work to train students who come after us in order to ensure the survival of the types of programs we want to continue to see.

We also suffer from the need to continually revise and rewrite our own historical accounts of these time periods. While many texts contain the same flaw, Connors's *Composition-Rhetoric* is a particular example. Connors's text is a valuable piece of research that has helped me immensely in my own study, but it does not always offer an accurate representation of the history of composition-rhetoric. Connors notes that during the time period after 1910, for example, "composition-rhetoric remained a scholarly backwater and a professional avocation, a drudgery, and a painful initiation ritual" (15). While that may have been the case in places that privileged a literature curriculum, my research shows this was not universally true. The current-traditional picture and the absorption of a progressive curriculum as a whole by current-traditionalism is not the only picture, and we need to consistently revise our history to reflect this. We need to even question histories such as the one I have written. Were there, for example, colleges and universities that remained progressive in their writing instruction, even through the 1930s and 1940s?[2] Only further research, mostly likely in archives, will tell.

However, if we are to have a more complete picture of our own history, we must continue to look. Throughout my work with Stevens and Hart, I have continually kept in mind Gail Griffin's words regarding her own work. "I've discovered that every story of every little college . . . reveals a foremother—a dean or principle or teacher, some woman of extraordinary gifts, power, and persistence who presides over some chapter of the institution's life and whose portrait hangs publicly somewhere on campus" (20). It is these foremothers who have also, most importantly, helped me enter into the profession of teaching as a woman and a composition instructor. As Jessica Enoch succinctly notes, "the work of these women should encourage us to reflect on and question the way we compose our own forms of rhetorical education" (175). Combining the history of progressivism and my research on female compositionists has provided me with a rich background from which to shape the teaching of composition. My research, with its focus on pedagogy, has forced me to ask myself what I want *my* classroom to look like, and to think about the relationship I want to foster with my students. It has helped me better understand both my place in the institution as a feminist teacher, and my place as a composition instructor. I want to honor my critical imaginings of Hart and Stevens in my daily practice, and in doing so, keep the traditions of progressive and feminist pedagogies alive and well.

Notes

Notes to Introduction

1. The proceedings of this conference are discussed in Mastrangelo and L'Eplattenier's "'Is it the Pleasure of this Conference to have another?': Women's Colleges Meeting and Talking about Writing in the Progressive Era."

2. I am using pragmatism and progressivism nearly interchangeably here. Pragmatism was a philosophical school of thought, whereas progressivism was a social movement. However, progressivism incorporated the key tents of pragmatism, such as the idea that practice is based on theory and the notion that validity of ideas is established through rigorous investigation. The key idea of pragmatism adopted by progressivism is the notion that ideas and experiences should be viewed in connection with one another (Goodman 2–3).

Notes to Chapter 1

1. Historians do not agree on specific dates for the Progressive Era. Elisabeth Israels Perry comments that "for me, it has come to mark the period from about the 1890s through the 1910s, but with the qualification that for some progressives the boundaries extended further" (3). I am framing my arguments around the late 1880s to the 1920s.

2. Russell, in his article "The Cooperation Movement," labels Dewey's approach as "organic" or "functionalist" progressivism (403). Labaree calls this form of progressivism "pedagogical progressivism" (275).

3. I am aware here that current-traditionalism is a term coined by modern scholars to describe what they believe to be problematic sets of practices. As a result, the term is often a conflicted and contested one. One of the difficulties here occurs in setting current-traditionalism in conversation with progressivism. Progressivism was a specific school of thought whereas current-traditionalism remains a construction. In addition, the current-traditionalism of the Progressive Era was seen as a positive response to a particular crisis. In retrospect, however, the administrative progressivism that

current-traditionalism espoused was detrimental to the development both of the individual student and the field of composition studies.

4. Conversely, in Deweyian progressivism, Fred Newton Scott used the term "composition-rhetoric," which, as Connors recalls, he defined as "a coherent tradition of conceptualizing the elements of correct and successful writing, trying to teach students how to find them in extant prose, and encouraging students to create them in their own prose" (*Composition-Rhetoric* 7). Connors sees this as more accurately reflecting a variety of approaches to nineteenth-century instruction. It is a much broader definition than current-traditionalism offers, and is derived from Scott and Denney's 1897 book by the same name. Connors uses "composition-rhetoric" to "identify specifically that form of rhetorical theory and practice devoted to written discourse" (6). I use the term "composition-rhetoric" throughout this text to indicate, as Connors did, the practices that "place writing centrally in rhetorical work" (6).

5. For information, see Martin J. Medhurst's "The History of Public Address as an Academic Study."

6. While Connors's definition of current-traditional pedagogy (see above) and the Harvard reports point out the tendency for correctness and rule enforcement, these do not point out the lengths to which instructors had gone to implement and enforce such rules. Progressive scholars such as Barnes ("The Reign of Red Ink," 1913) spoke out against what he saw as the overuse of red ink and the attention to grammatical and structural errors in student writing, which in his view had become so excessive by the early twentieth century as to be nonproductive. Barnes, in fact, noted that student writing was being "drowned," "stabbed," and "decapitated" by the red ink pen (163). Such violent images hardly connote productive results.

7. This view, including the language of disease, was later echoed by Shaughnessy in *Errors and Expectations*.

8. Dewey worked throughout his life to help change classroom practice at all levels of education, opening his first laboratory school in Chicago in 1896 and influencing the public schools in Gary, Indiana and Winnetka, Illinois, as well as the independent Teacher's College at Columbia. Eventually, the Progressive Movement in the schools led to such notable events as the founding of the Montessori schools at the pre-school level and open classroom systems at the elementary and high school level. Laboratory schools and open admissions institutions were also an outgrowth of Dewey's visionary thinking. Thus, there has been consistent attention to the tradition of Deweyian progressivism in the link between theory and practice.

9. A lack of standardization of any kind, and lack of content and discipline led to equally problematic forms of education for Dewey. The Play School developed in the 1920s, for example, overstepped the boundaries of expressivism and Deweyian progressivism by simply providing students with

materials, but no lesson, and expecting students to work with those materials to reach some conclusion, but with no assistance from the teacher. In such a situation, structure was altogether missing, although some traditional content was still included (Cremin 234).

10. Later scholars such as Paulo Freire, with his notions of liberatory pedagogy, and Ira Shor, with his theories about critical pedagogy, both echo Dewey on these points.

11. The definition of "feminist" that I am using here is a complex one, derived mostly from post-structural feminist definitions where feminism advocates for social change, works to solve injustice, and sees human beings as socially, culturally, and historically situated and constantly evolving. Dewey's pragmatist belief in transaction supports this.

Notes to Chapter 2

1. While many current scholars are more aware of Scott than they used to be, Stewart noted in "Rediscovering Fred Newton Scott" that in 1978, of seventy-four people he informally surveyed, only seven had ever heard of him, and of those, only one had ever read any of Scott's work (539). Although I suspect the numbers would be at least somewhat better now, this is both surprising and unfortunate, given the amount of successful work Scott accomplished during his lifetime to improve the situation of rhetoric and composition instruction at the university level.

2. For more information about women in the graduate programs at the University of Michigan, see Mastrangelo, "Building a Dinosaur From the Bones: Fred Newton Scott and Women's Progressive Era Graduate Work at the University of Michigan."

3. There are some discrepancies in the number of graduate students Scott taught. Shaw's history of the University of Michigan lists 140 students with master's degrees and twenty-five with PhDs. Stewart and Stewart claim that there were 150 MAs and twenty-five PhDs. The records I examined from the Department of English Language and Literature list 125 MA degrees and twenty-five PhDs between 1894 and 1926.

4. For more information on Buck, see Bordelon or Campbell.

5. Vassar was founded in 1865, Smith and Wellesley in 1875, and Bryn Mawr in 1889. Barnard, founded as an annex of Columbia in 1889, and Radcliffe, founded as an annex of Harvard in 1879, came into existence as Harvard and Columbia respectively struggled to avoid co-education. Mount Holyoke, founded in 1837, was technically the first of the Seven Sisters, although the seminary did not formally become a college until 1888.

6. More information on the conference is available in Mastrangelo and L'Eplattenier's "'Is it the Pleasure of This Conference to Have Another?': Women Meeting and Talking about Writing."

Notes to Chapter 3

1. The female seminaries and academies had a strong tradition of teaching elements of written composition. Of 162 seminaries Woody reviewed, course offerings from 1742–1871 revealed that ninety-six institutions offered composition, 139 taught grammar, and 121 included rhetoric in their curriculum.

2. Woody's *A History of Women's Education in the United States* lists Blair, Newman, and Whately among the textbooks routinely mentioned in Academy and Seminary Catalogs (1780–1870) (Vol. I, 560). As well, they are cited on his list of textbooks mentioned in women's college catalogs since 1850 (Vol. II, 474).

3. According to alumnae records, Tingley was not part of the majority of Mount Holyoke women who taught after graduation. Documentation remains unclear as to whether or not she worked at all between her graduation in 1855 and her marriage in 1860, but she never listed teaching as a paid or volunteer occupation on alumnae reports. Perhaps her experience in the remedial spelling class discouraged her (Tingley, Alumnae Biographical File). Department meeting records as late as the 1920s still recommend students for "conditioning" in areas such as spelling and outlining.

4. This was reflective of the trend in women's higher education across the United States. Mabel Newcomer, in *A Century of Higher Education for American Women*, notes that in 1880 there were forty thousand women enrolled in colleges and universities across the United States. By 1890 that number had increased to 56,000, and by 1900 it had more than doubled to 85,000 (46).

5. Fred Newton Scott is typically credited with the first course in journalism in 1890. This course would have been in place when Stevens attended the University of Michigan. However, her implementation of the course at Mount Holyoke puts her on the cutting edge of a new field. Berlin also notes that, of the colleges he surveyed, only Mount Holyoke and Harvard offered courses in playwriting (56).

6. For more information on debate at Mount Holyoke, see Mastrangelo, "Learning from the Past: Composition, Rhetoric, and Debate at Mount Holyoke College."

7. I am aware that expressivism is a contested term in English studies, but there are several characteristics that tend to be common to expressivist pedagogies, including a focus on process and a commitment to student-centered writing pedagogy. Often this includes writing about personal experiences in order to help students develop their own writing "voices." All of these characteristics are clearly present in Stevens's pedagogy.

8. Interestingly enough, Northrup's *Report* portrays such conservatism as a very positive thing, whereas here the quote serves its purpose to show

that Ham's agenda would have been more conservative than what Mount Holyoke was used to, and what they considered improvement to their system. Northrup himself was a Yale graduate.

9. Margaret Ball, Mount Holyoke College faculty from 1906 to 1943, had taken over the debate activities in the 1920s. Her retirement in 1943 is coincidental with the 1945 vote to abandon the debate class.

NOTES TO CHAPTER 4

1. Hart did actually publish other articles. One, titled "The Relation of College Experience to Present Social Demands," was published in the *Journal of the Association of Collegiate Alumnae* and focused on women's roles as college students rather than on English studies. A second, "Russia from an American Point of View," was a reflection on a trip she had taken, and was published in *Home Progress*.

2. Women were finally added to the Board of Trustees of Mount Holyoke in 1884, but only at the insistence of the alumnae (Stow 278).

3. The elocution program remained relatively static during the beginning of the nineteenth century. Only three courses are listed (Elocution 1, Training of the Body and Voice; Elocution 2, Training of the Body and Voice: Expression; and Elocution 3, Reading of Shakespeare). All of the courses were taught by the same instructor for many years. The only course text listed is King's *Graduated Exercises in Articulation*, which is listed in the Course Catalog in 1911–12.

4. Baker has been placed squarely as a current-traditionalist by scholars such as Connors, although Connors's assertion is based almost solely on Baker's textbook, *The Principles of Argumentation*. Scholars such as Bordelon and Crowley have recently argued that Baker was actually using progressive methods, especially workshopping of papers.

NOTES TO CHAPTER 5

1. The decline of the women's movement was partially attributed to the shift in focus to World War I, and after 1920, to the fact that the women's movement became less organized and focused once suffrage was achieved (Clifford 2).

2. Thomas Masters's *Practicing Writing: Postwar Discourse of Freshman English* looks at the practice of teaching writing from 1947–1963, but this still leaves a large time gap of the 1930s and 1940s that needs in-depth exploration.

Works Cited

Adams, Katherine. *A Group of Their Own: College Writing Courses and American Women Writers, 1880–1940*. Albany: SUNY P, 2001. Print.

—. *Progressive Politics and the Training of America's Persuaders*. Mahwah, NJ: Lawrence Erlbaum, 1999. Print.

Allmendinger, David F. "Mount Holyoke Students Encounter the Need for Life-Planning, 1837–1850." *History of Education Quarterly* (Spring 1979): 27–46. Print.

Alridge, Derrick P. "Of Victorianism, Civilization, and Progressivism: The Educational Ideas of Anna Julia Cooper and W.E.B. Du Bois, 1892–1940." *History of Education Quarterly* 47.4 (2007): 416–46. Print.

Antler, Joyce. *The Educated Woman and Professionalization: The Struggle for a New Feminine Identity, 1890-1920*. New York: Garland, 1987.

Aronowitz, Stanley, and Henry A. Giroux. *Education Still Under Siege*. Westport, CT: Bergin and Garvey, 1993. Print.

Baker, George P. and Henry Huntington. *Principles of Argumentation*. Boston, MA: Ginn and Co., 1895. Print.

Barnes, Walter F. "The Reign of Red Ink." *English Journal* (1912): 158–65. Print.

Bates, Katherine Lee. "English at Wellesley College." *The Dial* (October 16, 1894): 219–21. Print.

Berlin, James. *Rhetoric and Reality: Writing Instruction in American Colleges, 1900– 1985*. Carbondale: Southern Illinois UP, 1987. Print.

—. *Writing Instruction in Nineteenth-Century American Colleges*. Carbondale: Southern Illinois UP, 1984. Print.

Bizzell, Patricia and Mark Herzberg. *The Rhetorical Tradition: Readings from Classical Times to the Present*. New York: Bedford/St. Martin's, 2000. Print.

Blair, Hugh. *Lectures in Rhetoric and Belles Lettres*. Ed. Harold Harding. Carbondale: Southern Illinois UP, 1965. Print.

Bordelon, Suzanne. "The 'Advance' Toward Democratic Administration: Laura Johnson Wylie and Gertrude Buck of Vassar College." *Historical Studies of Writing Program Administration: Individuals, Communities, and the Formation of a Discipline*. Ed. Barbara L'Eplattenier and Lisa Mastrangelo. West Lafayette, IN: Parlor Press, 2004. 91–116. Print.

—. *A Feminist Legacy: The Rhetoric and Pedagogy of Gertrude Buck.* Carbondale: Southern Illinois UP, 2009. Print.

—. "A Reassessment of George Pierce Baker's *The Principle of Argumentation*: Minimizing the Use of Formal Logic in Favor of Practical Approaches." *College Composition and Communication* 57.4 (2006): 763–88. Print.

Bowles, Samuel and Herbert Gintis. *Schooling in Capitalist America.* New York: Basic Books, 1976. Print.

Brereton, John C., ed. *The Origins of Composition Studies in the American College, 1875–1925.* Pittsburgh, PA: U of Pittsburgh P, 1995. Print.

Briggs, LeBaron Russell. "The Correction of Bad English as a Requirement for Admission to Harvard College." *The Academy* 5 (1890): 395. Print.

Brody, Miriam. *Manly Writing: Gender, Rhetoric, and the Rise of Composition.* Carbondale: Southern Illinois UP, 1993. Print.

Buck, Gertrude. *The Metaphor: A Study in the Psychology of Rhetoric.* Diss. University of Michigan, 1898. *Contributions to Rhetorical Theory* 5. Ed. Fred Newton Scott. Ann Arbor, MI: Inland Press, 1899. Print.

Cameron, Ardis. *Radicals of the Worst Sort: Laboring Women in Lawrence, Massachusetts, 1860–1912.* Urbana: U of Illinois P, 1993. Print.

Campbell, Joanne. "Women's Work, Worthy Work: Composition Instruction at Vassar College, 1897–1922." *Constructing Rhetorical Education.* Ed. Marie Secor and Davida Charney. Carbondale: Southern Illinois UP, 1992. 26–42. Print.

Chappell, Dorothy Havens. "Sophie Chantal Hart." *The Wellesley Magazine* (October 1937): 12. Print.

Cheek, Mary Ashby, Helen Griffith, and John Martyn Warbeke. "Clara Frances Stevens." *Mount Holyoke Alumnae Quarterly* Vol. XVIII (February 1935): 221–28. Print.

"Clara Frances Stevens, Ph.M." *Llamarada* (1899): 15–16. Mount Holyoke Archives and Special Collections, South Hadley, MA. Print.

Clark, Suzanne. "Argument and Composition." *Feminism and Composition Studies: In Other Words.* Ed. Susan Jarratt and Lynne Worsham. New York: MLA, 1998. 94–99. Print.

Clifford, Geraldine Jonçich. *Lone Voyagers: Academic Women in Coeducational Institutions, 1870–1937.* New York: Feminist Press, 1989. Print.

Colby, June Rose. *Literature and Life in School.* Boston, MA: Houghton, Mifflin and Company, 1906. Print.

Connors, Robert. *Composition-Rhetoric.* Pittsburgh, PA: U of Pittsburgh P, 1997. Print.

—. "Women's Reclamation of Rhetoric in Nineteenth-Century America." *Feminine Principles and Women's Experience in American Composition and Rhetoric.* Ed. Louise Wetherbee Phelps and Janet A. Emig. Pittsburgh, PA: U of Pittsburgh P, 1995. 67–90. Print.

Converse, Florence. *The Story of Wellesley*. Boston, MA: Little, Brown, and Company, 1915. Print.

—. *Wellesley College: A Chronicle of the Years 1875–1938*. Wellesley, MA: Hathaway House Bookshop, 1939. Print.

Conway, Katherine. "Woman Suffrage and the History of Rhetoric at the Seven Sisters Colleges, 1865–1919." *Reclaiming Rhetorica: Women in the Rhetorical Tradition*. Ed. Andrea Lunsford. Pittsburgh, PA: U of Pittsburgh P, 1995. 203–26. Print.

Cooper, Lane. "On the Teaching of Written Composition." *Education* 30 (1910): 421–30. Print.

Corbett, Edward P.J. *Classical Rhetoric for the Modern Student-Second Edition*. New York: Oxford University Press, 1971. Print.

Corcoran, James. Letter to Fred Newton Scott. Fred Newton Scott Papers. Box 1, Correspondence 1920. Bentley Historical Library, The University of Michigan, Ann Arbor. Print.

Cremin, Lawrence. *The Transformation of the School*. New York: Alfred A. Knopf, 1964. Print.

Crocco, Margaret Smith, Petra Munro, and Kathleen Weiler. *Pedagogies of Resistance: Women Educator Activists, 1880–1960*. New York: Teachers College Press, 1999. Print.

Croley, Herbert. "Individual vs. Collective Education." *Social History of American Education Vol. II: 1860 to the Present*. Ed. Rena L. Vassar. Chicago, IL: Rand McNally & Company, 1965. 246–56. Print.

Crowley, Sharon. *Composition in the University*. Pittsburgh, PA: U of Pittsburgh P, 1998. Print.

Curti, Merle. *The Social Ideas of American Educators*. Paterson, NJ: Pageant Books, 1959. Print.

Davidson, Cathy, and Linda Wagner-Martin, eds. *The Oxford Companion to Women's Writing in the United States*. New York: Oxford UP, 1995. 211–12. Print.

Dealey, Hermione. "A Comparative Study of the Curricula of Wellesley, Smith, and Vassar Colleges." *The Pedagogical Seminary* (September 1915): 347–75. Print.

—. "College Curricula and Interests of College Women." *School and Society* 10.245 (1919): 294–96. Print.

Decker, Joe F. "The Progressive Era and the World War I Draft." *OAH Magazine of History* 1.3–4 (1986): 15–18. Print.

Dewey, John. *Democracy and Education*. New York: The Free Press, 1966. Print

—. *Experience and Education*. New York: Touchstone Press, 1977. Print.

—. "Fred Newton Scott." *The Early Works, 1882–1898*. Ed. Jo Ann Boydston. Carbondale: Southern Illinois UP, 1971. Print.

—."Mediocrity and Individuality." *The New Republic* 33 (December 6, 1922): 35–37. Print.

—. *The Middle Works, 1899–1924*. Ed. Jo Ann Boydston. Carbondale: Southern Illinois UP, 1983. Print.

—. "The Need for a Philosophy of Education." *John Dewey on Education*. Ed. Reginald Archambault. Chicago, IL: U of Chicago P, 1964. 3–14. Print.

—. "Progressive Education and the Science of Education." *John Dewey on Education*. Ed. Reginald Archambault. Chicago, IL: U of Chicago P, 1964. 169–81. Print.

Downey, June Etta. *The Creative Imagination*. New York: Harcourt Brace, 1929. Print.

Duran, Jane. "The Intersection of Feminism and Pragmatism." *Hypatia* 8.2 (1993): 159–71. Print.

Edson, C.H. "Curriculum Change during the Progressive Era." *Educational Leadership* (October 1978): 64–69. Print.

Eisenmann, Linda. "Creating a Framework for Interpreting U.S. Women's Educational History: Lessons from Historical Lexicography." *History of Education* 30.5 (2001): 453–70. Print.

Elbow, Peter. *Writing Without Teachers*. New York: Oxford UP, 1973. Print.

Enoch, Jessica. *Refiguring Rhetorical Education: Women Teaching African American, Native American, and Chicano/a Students, 1865–1911*. Carbondale: Southern Illinois UP, 2008. Print.

Emig, Janet. *The Web of Meaning*. New York: Boynton/Cook, 1983. Print.

Evans, Marian MacGown. "Miss Clara Stevens: A Tribute." Leaflet. Mount Holyoke College Archives and Special Collections, South Hadley, MA. Print.

Faigley, Lester. "Nonacademic Writing: The Social Perspective." *Writing in Nonacademic Settings*. Ed. Lee Odell and Dixie Goswami. New York: The Guilford Press, 1985. 231–48. Print.

Fishman, Stephen M. "Explicating Our Tacit Tradition: John Dewey and Composition Studies." *College Composition and Communication* 44:3 (1993): 315–30. Print.

Fley, Jo Ann. "LeBaron Russell Briggs: He Meant Harvard." *Journal of the NAWDAC* 41.1 (1977): 21–24. Print.

Flower, Linda, and John Hayes. "A Cognitive Process Theory of Writing." *College Composition and Communication* 32 (1981): 365–87. Print.

Freire, Paulo. *The Pedagogy of the Oppressed*. New York: Continuum Press, 1996. Print.

Genung, John Franklin. *The Practical Elements of Rhetoric*. Boston, MA: Ginn and Company, 1886. Print.

Glenn, Cheryl. *Rhetoric Retold: Regendering the Tradition from Antiquity Through the Renaissance*. Carbondale: Southern Illinois UP, 1997. Print.

Godkin, E. L. "The Illiteracy of American Boys." *Educational Review* 13 (1897): 1–9. Print.

Gold, David. *Rhetoric at the Margins: Revising the History of Writing Instruction in American Colleges, 1873–1947.* Carbondale: Southern Illinois UP, 2008. Print.

Goodman, Russell. *Pragmatism: A Contemporary Reader.* New York: Routledge, 1995. Print.

Gordon, Lynn. *Gender and Higher Education in the Progressive Era.* New Haven, CT: Yale UP, 1990. Print.

Greenough, James Jay. "The English Question." *Atlantic Monthly* (May 1893): 656–62. Print.

—. "The Present Requirements for Admission to Harvard College." *Atlantic Monthly* (May 1892): 671–77. Print.

Griffin, Gail B. *Calling: Essay on Teaching in the Mother Tongue.* Pasadena, CA: Trilogy Books, 1992. Print.

Guild, Marion Pelton. "Wellesley College." *The Outlook* (July 1894): 99. Print.

Haight, Elizabeth Hazelton. "Pleasant Possibles in Lady Professors." *The Journal of the Association of Collegiate Alumnae* 11 (September 1917): 10–17. Print.

Hairston, Maxine. "The Winds of Change: Thomas Kuhn and the Revolution in the Teaching of Writing." *College Composition and Communication* 33 (February 1982): 76–88. Print.

Ham, Roswell. Personal Papers. Mount Holyoke Archives and Special Collections, South Hadley, MA. Print.

Harmston, Richard K. "Closing the Department of Rhetoric at Michigan: A Matter of Politics, Place and Power." Unpublished Manuscript. Bentley Historical Library, The University of Michigan, Ann Arbor, 1985. Print.

Hart, John S. *A Manual of Composition and Rhetoric.* Philadelphia, PA: Eldredge and Brother, 1895. Print.

Hart, Sophie Chantal. Alumnae Biographical File. Radcliffe College Archives and Special Collections, Boston, MA. Print.

—. "English Composition—An Interpretation." *The Wellesley Magazine* (June 1937): 372–74. Print.

—. "English in the College." *The School Review* 10 (1902): 364–73. Print.

—. Personal Papers. Wellesley College Archives and Special Collections, Wellesley, MA.

—. "Relation of College Experience to Present Social Demands." *Journal of the Association of Collegiate Alumnae* 3.18 (1908): 56. Print.

—. "Russia from an American Point of View" *Home Progress* 4 (July 1915): 1096–1102. Print.

Hartley, James. *Mary Lyon: Documents and Writings.* South Hadley, MA: Doorlight Publications, 2008. Print.

Hill, Adams Sherman. *The Principles of Rhetoric, and Their Application*. New York: Harper and Brothers, 1878. Print.

Hobbs, Catherine, ed. *Nineteenth-Century Women Learn to Write*. Charlottesville: The UP of Virginia, 1995. Print.

Hopkins, Edwin. *The Labor and the Cost of the Teaching of English in Colleges and Secondary Schools with Especial Reference to English Composition*. Chicago, IL: NCTE, 1923. Print.

Horowitz, Helen. *Alma Mater*. New York: Knopf, 1984. Print.

Hughes, James Monroe, and Frederick Schultz. *Education in America*. New York: UP of America, 1985. Print.

Hunt, Lynn. "History as Gesture; or, The Scandal of History" *Consequences of Theory*. Ed. Jonathan Arac and Barbara Johnson. Baltimore, MD: Johns Hopkins UP, 1991. 91–107. Print.

Jarratt, Susan. "Feminism and Composition: The Case for Conflict." *Contending With Words: Composition and Rhetoric in a Postmodern Age*. Ed. Patricia Harkin and John Schilb. New York: MLA, 1991. 105–23. Print.

Johnson, Nan. *Nineteenth-Century Rhetoric in North America*. Carbondale: Southern Illinois UP, 1991. Print.

Johnson, Ruth. Personal Papers. Mount Holyoke Archives and Special Collections, South Hadley, MA. Print.

Keith, William. *Democracy as Discussion: Civic Education and the American Forum Movement*. New York: Lexington Books, 2007. Print.

Kerlinger, Fred N. "Progressivism and Traditionalism: Basic Educational Attitudes." *The School Review* 66.1 (1958): 80–92.

King, Samuel A. *Graduated Exercises in Articulation*. New York: Small, Maynard, & Company, 1906. Print.

Kirsch, Gesa E. and Jacqueline Jones Royster. "Feminist Rhetorical Practices: In Search of Excellence." *College Composition and Communication* 61.4 (2010): 640–672. Print.

Kitzhaber, Albert. *Rhetoric in American Colleges, 1850–1900*. Dallas, TX: Southern Methodist UP, 1990. Print.

Knoblauch, Cy, and Lil Brannon. *Rhetorical Traditions and the Teaching of Writing*. Portsmouth, NH: Heinemann, 1984. Print.

Labaree, David. "Progressivism, Schools and Schools of Education: An American Romance." *Paedagogica Historica* 41.1–2 (2005): 275–88. Print.

Lebsock, Suzanne. "Women and American Politics, 1880–1920." *Women, Politics, and Change*. Ed. L. Tilly and P. Gurin. New York: Russell Sage Foundation, 1990. 35–62. Print.

Lemons, J. Stanley. *The Woman Citizen: Social Feminism in the 1920s*. Chicago, IL: U of Chicago P, 1973. Print.

Leonard, Sterling. *Current English Usage*. Chicago, IL: Inland Press, 1932. Print.

—. *The Doctrine of Correctness in English Usage, 1700–1800*. U of Wisconsin Studies in Language and Literature 25, 1929. Print.
Lewes, George Henry. *Principles of Success in Literature*. Boston, MA: Allyn and Bacon, 1917. Print.
Livingston, James. *Pragmatism, Feminism, and Democracy*. New York: Routledge, 2001. Print.
Lockwood, Helen Drusilla. Letters to Parents. 25 February 1912. Vassar Archives and Special Collections, Poughkeepsie, NY. Print.
Logan, Shirley Wilson. *We Are Coming: The Persuasive Discourse of Nineteenth-Century Black Women*. Carbondale: Southern Illinois UP, 1999. Print.
Lunsford, Andrea, ed. *Reclaiming Rhetorica: Women in the Rhetorical Tradition*. Pittsburgh, PA: U of Pittsburgh P, 1995. Print.
Mahin, Helen Ogden. 1929. "Half-Lights." *The Fred Newton Scott Anniversary Papers*. Freeport, NY: Books for Libraries Press, 1968. 1–4. Print.
Markowitz, Linda. "Unmasking Moral Dichotomies: Can Feminist Pedagogy Overcome Student Resistance?" *Gender and Education* 17.1 (2005): 39–55. Print.
Masters, Thomas. *Practicing Writing: Postwar Discourse of Freshman English*. Pittsburgh, PA: U of Pittsburgh P, 2004. Print.
Mastrangelo, Lisa. "Building a Dinosaur from the Bones: Fred Newton Scott and Women's Progressive Era Graduate Work at the University of Michigan." *Rhetoric Review* 24.4 (2005): 403–20. Print.
—."Learning from the Past: Composition, Rhetoric, and Debate at Mount Holyoke College." *Rhetoric Review* 18 (Fall 1999): 46–64. Print.
Mastrangelo, Lisa, and Barbara L'Eplattenier. "'Is it the Pleasure of this Conference to Have Another?': Women's Colleges Meeting and Talking about Writing in the Progressive Era." *Historical Studies of Writing Program Administration: Individuals, Communities, and the Formation of a Discipline*. Ed. Barbara L'Eplattenier and Lisa Mastrangelo. West Lafayette, IN: Parlor Press, 2004. 117–143. Print.
Medhurst, Martin J. "The History of Public Address as an Academic Study." Unpublished manuscript. Print.
Middleton, Sue. *Educating Feminists: Life Histories and Pedagogy*. New York: Teachers College Press, 1993. Print.
Miller, Susan. *Rescuing the Subject: A Critical Introduction to Rhetoric and the Writer*. Carbondale: Southern Illinois UP, 1989. Print.
Mount Holyoke College. English Department Papers. Archives and Special Collections, South Hadley, MA. Print.
Muncy, Robyn. "The Ambiguous Legacies of Women's Progressivism." *OAH Magazine of History* (Spring 1999): 15–19. Print.

Murray, Donald "Teach Writing as a Process not a Product." *Cross-Talk in Comp Theory*. Ed. Victor Villanueva. Urbana, IL: NCTE, 2003. 3–6. Print.

Murray, Lindley. *An English Grammar*. New York: Thomas Wilson, 1842. Print.

Newcomer, Mabel. *A Century of Higher Education for American Women*. New York: Harper Press, 1959. Print.

Newman, Samuel P. *A Practical System of Rhetoric*. Andover, MA: Gould & Newman, 1839. Print.

Nietzsche, Frederick. *The Will to Power*. New York: Random House Books, 1968. Print.

Northrup, Cyrus. "Yale and Its Relation to the Development of the Country." *Report of the Commissioner of Education* 1 (1902): 588–94. Print.

Overstreet, H. A. *Influencing Human Behavior*. New York: Norton, 1925. Print.

Palmieri, Patricia A. "Here Was Fellowship: A Social Portrait of Academic Women at Wellesley College, 1895–1920." *History of Education Quarterly* 23:2 (1983): 195–214. Print.

—. *In Adamless Eden: The Community of Women Faculty at Wellesley*. New Haven, CT: Yale UP, 1995. Print.

—. "Symmetrical Womanhood: The Educational Ideology of Activism at Wellesley." *Academe* 81.4 (1995): 16–20. Print.

Payne, William Morton, ed. *English in American Universities*. Boston, MA: Heath and Company, 1895. Print.

Perry, Bliss. "The Life of A College Professor." *Scribners* 22 (1897): 512–18. Print.

Perry, Elisabeth Israels. "The Changing Meanings of 'The Progressive Era.'" *OAH Magazine of History* 13.3 (1999): 3–4. Print.

Phelps, Louise Wetherbee, and Janet Emig. *Feminine Principles and Women's Experience in American Composition and Rhetoric*. Pittsburgh, PA: U of Pittsburgh P, 1995. Print.

Popken, Randall. "Edwin Hopkins and the Costly Labor of Composition Teaching." *College Composition and Communication* 55.4 (2004): 618–41. Print.

Potter, Adaline. Personal Interview. 14 November 1998.

Prentiss, Mary Eleanor. "Sophie Chantal Hart: Professor of Rhetoric and Composition, Emeritus." *The Wellesley Magazine* (February 1949): 182–83. Print.

Quackenbos, George Payn. *First Lessons in Composition*. New York: D. Appleton & Co., 1863. Print.

Quinn, Patrick. Letter to President Clapp. 1959. Special Collections, Wellesley College Archives, Wellesley, MA. Print.

Rankin, Thomas. English Department Annual Report, 1931–32. Department of English. Carleton College Archives and Special Collections, Northfield, MN. Print.

Riis, Jacob. *How the Other Half Lives*. Cambridge, MA: Belknap Press, 1970. Print.

Ritchie, Joy, and Kate Ronald. "Riding Long Coattails, Subverting Tradition." *Feminism and Composition Studies: In Other Words*. Ed. Susan Jarratt and Lynn Worsham. New York: MLA, 1988. 217–38. Print.

Rodgers, Daniel. "In Search of Progressivism." *Reviews in American History* 10.4 (1982): 113–32. Print.

Russell, David R. "The Cooperation Movement: Language Across the Curriculum and Mass Education, 1900–1930." *Research in the Teaching of English* 23.4 (1989): 399–423. Print.

—. *Writing in the Academic Disciplines, 1870–1990*. Carbondale: Southern Illinois UP, 1991. Print.

Rynbrandt, Linda J. *Caroline Bartlett Crane and Progressive Reform: Social Housekeeping as Sociology*. New York: Garland Publishing, 1999. Print.

Schell, Eileen. "The Costs of Caring: 'Feminism' and Contingent Women Workers in Composition." *Feminism and Composition Studies: In Other Words*. Ed. Susan Jarratt and Lynn Worsham. New York: MLA, 1988. 74–93. Print.

Schneider, Dorothy, and Carl Schneider. *American Women in the Progressive Era, 1900–1920*. New York: Anchor Books, 1993. Print.

Schutz, Aaron. "John Dewey's Conundrum: Can Democratic Schools Empower?" *Teachers College Record* 103.2 (2001): 267–302. Print.

Scott, Fred Newton, and Joseph Villiers Denney. *Aphorisms for Teachers of English Composition*. Boston, MA: Allyn & Bacon, 1905. Print.

Scott, Fred Newton, George Rice Carpenter, and Franklin Thomas Baker. *The Teaching of English in the Elementary and Secondary School*. New York: Longmans, Green, and Co., 1903. Print.

Scott, Fred Newton. Diaries and Daybooks. Bentley Historical Library, The University of Michigan, Ann Arbor. Print.

—. "Efficiency for Efficiency's Sake." *The Standard of American Speech*. New York: Allyn & Bacon, 1926. Print.

—. "English Composition as a Mode of Behavior." *English Journal* 11 (October 1922): 463–73. Print.

—. "English at the University of Michigan." *English in American Universities*. Ed. William Morton Payne. Boston, MA: D.C. Heath, 1895. Print.

—. Personal Correspondence. Bentley Historical Library, The University of Michigan. Ann Arbor. Print.

—. "The Report on the Entrance Exams in English." *Educational Review* 20 (October 1900): 289–94. Print.

—. "Two Ideals of Composition Teaching." *The Standard of American Speech*. New York: Allyn & Bacon, 1926. Print.

—. "What the West Wants in Preparatory English." *The School Review* 17 (January 1909): 10–20. Print.

Seigfried, Charlene Haddock. *Pragmatism and Feminism*. Chicago, IL: U of Chicago P, 1996. Print.

Sharer, Wendy. *Vote and Voice: Women's Organizations and Political Literacy, 1915–1930*. Carbondale: Southern Illinois UP, 2004. Print.

Shaw, Wilfred, ed. *The University of Michigan: An Encyclopedic Survey*. New York: Harcourt, Brace, & Howe, 1920. Print.

Shaugnessey, Mina P. *Errors and Expectations*. New York: Oxford UP, 1977. Print.

Sheils, Merrill. "Why Johnny Can't Write." *Newsweek* 8 December 1975: 58–62, 65. Print.

Shor, Ira. *Critical Teaching and Everyday Life*. Chicago, IL: U of Chicago P, 1987. Print.

Simmons, Sue Carter. "Constructing Writers: Barrett Wendell's Pedagogy at Harvard." *College Composition and Communication* 46.3 (1995): 327–50. Print.

Smith, Donald. "Origin and Development of Departments of Speech." *History of Speech Education in America*. Ed. Karl Wallace. New York: Appleton-Century-Crofts, 1954. 447–70. Print.

Smith, Shirley. "Fred Newton Scott as a Teacher." *Michigan Alumnus* (4 February 1933): 279–80. Print.

Snell, Ada F. "History of English Studies in Mount Holyoke Seminary and College." Unpublished typescript, 1942. English Department Records. Mount Holyoke Archives and Special Collections, South Hadley, MA. Print.

—. *Pause. Contributions to Rhetorical Theory*. Ed. F. N. Scott. Vol. 8. Ann Arbor, MI: Ann Arbor Press, 1918. Print.

Spencer, Herbert. *The Philosophy of Style*. Boston, MA: Allyn and Bacon, 1892. Print.

Sproule, J. Michael. *Propaganda and Democracy: The American Experience of Media and Mass Persuasion*. New York: Cambridge UP, 1997. Print.

Stevens, Clara F. 1924 Alumnae Survey. University of Michigan Alumnae Association: Box 109. Bentley Historical Library, The University of Michigan, Ann Arbor. Print.

—. "A Suggestive Report." *The Journal of Pedagogy* 19 (June 1907): 251–54. Print.

—. Alumnae Survey of 1927. Mount Holyoke College Archives and Special Collections, South Hadley, MA. Print.

—. "College English." *English Education* (October 1906): 101–11. Print.

—. "The Ethics of English Work." *New England Association of Teachers of English, Leaflet No. 14* (March 1, 1903). Print.
—. Personal Papers. Mount Holyoke Archives and Special Collections, South Hadley, MA. Print.
Stewart, Donald C. "Rediscovering Fred Newton Scott." *College English* 40 (1979): 539–47. Print.
—. Personal Interview with Jean Paul Slusser. 9 August 1980. Donald C. Stewart Papers, Box 3. Bentley Historical Library, The University of Michigan, Ann Arbor. Print.
Stewart, Donald C., and Patricia L. Stewart. *The Life and Legacy of Fred Newton Scott.* Pittsburgh, PA: U of Pittsburgh P, 1997. Print.
Stow, Sarah D. *History of Mount Holyoke Seminary, South Hadley, Mass. During Its First Half Century, 1837–1887.* Springfield, MA: Springfield Printing Company, 1887. Print.
Strauss, Louis. "Regents Merge Two Departments." *The Michigan Alumnus* 36 (February 8, 1930): 331–32, 336. Print.
Sugg, Redding. *MotherTeacher: The Feminization of American Education.* Charlottesville: UP of Virginia, 1978. Print.
Thomas, Susan Elizabeth. *Part of a Larger Whole: Fred Newton Scott and the Progressive Education Movement.* Diss. Georgia State University, 2002. Print.
Tingley, Nell. Alumnae Biographical File. Mount Holyoke Archives and Special Collections, South Hadley, MA. Print.
Tyack, David. *Turning Points in American Educational History.* Waltham, MA: Blaisdell Publishing, 1967. Print.
Tyack, David, and Larry Cuban. *Tinkering Towards Utopia: A Century of Public School Reform.* Cambridge, MA: Harvard UP, 1995. Print.
University of Michigan Course Catalog. 1908–1909. Bentley Historical Library, The University of Michigan, Ann Arbor. Print.
Vassar College Catalog. 1876–1877. Vassar College Archives and Special Collections, Poughkeepsie, NY. Print.
Wagner, Joanne. "'Intelligent Members or Restless Disturbers': Women's Rhetorical Styles, 1880–1920." *Reclaiming Rhetorica: Women in the Rhetorical Tradition.* Ed. Andrea Lunsford. Pittsburgh, PA: U of Pittsburgh P, 1995. 185–202. Print.
Walker, Danna L., Margaretha Geertsema, and Barbara Barnett. "Inverting the Inverted Pyramid: A Conversation about the Use of Feminist Theories to Teach Journalism." *Feminist Teacher* 19.3 (2009): 177–94. Print.
Ward, Lester Frank. *Dynamic Sociology,* Volume II. New York: D. Appleton and Company, 1920. Print.
Weedon, Chris. *Feminist Practice and Poststructuralist Theory.* Cambridge, MA: Blackwell Publishers, Inc., 1997. Print.

Weeks, Ruth Mary. 1924 Alumnae Survey. University of Michigan Alumnae Association: Box 109. Bentley Historical Library, The University of Michigan, Ann Arbor. Print.

Wellesley College, Course Catalogs. 1903–1904. Wellesley College Archives and Special Collections, Wellesley, MA. Print.

Wellesley College, Course Catalogs. 1926–1927. Wellesley College Archives and Special Collections, Wellesley, MA. Print.

Wellesley College, English Department Papers. Wellesley College Archives and Special Collections, Wellesley, MA. Print.

Wellesley College, President's Annual Report, 1889. Wellesley College Archives and Special Collections, Wellesley, MA. Print.

Wellesley College, President's Annual Report, 1890. Wellesley College Archives and Special Collections, Wellesley, MA. Print.

Wellesley College, President's Annual Report, 1892. Wellesley College Archives and Special Collections, Wellesley, MA. Print.

Wellesley College, President's Annual Report, 1893. Wellesley College Archives and Special Collections, Wellesley, MA. Print.

Wellesley College, President's Annual Report, 1895. Wellesley College Archives and Special Collections, Wellesley, MA. Print.

Wellesley College, President's Annual Report, 1909. Wellesley College Archives and Special Collections, Wellesley, MA. Print.

Wellesley College, President's Annual Report, 1912. Wellesley College Archives and Special Collections, Wellesley, MA. Print.

Whately, Richard. *Elements of Rhetoric*. Ed. Douglas Ehninger. Carbondale: Southern Illinois UP, 1963. Print.

Wolcott, Emily. Personal Correspondence. 9 March 1903. Kelso House Collection, Kent State University, Department of Special Collections and Archives, Kent, OH. Print.

Woody, Thomas. *A History of Women's Education in the United States in Two Volumes*. New York: The Science Press, 1929. Print.

Yost, Mary. 1924 University of Michigan Alumnae Survey. Bentley Historical Library, The University of Michigan, Ann Arbor. Print.

Young, Richard. "Paradigms and Problems: Needed Research in Rhetorical Invention." *Research on Composition*. Ed. Charles R. Cooper and Lee Odell. Urbana, IL: NCTE, 1978. 29–48. Print.

Index

academic: argument, 31; Wellesley Council, 102, 129
academic discourse, 30
activism, 32, 65, 96, 103
Adams, Charles Francis, 16
Addams, Jane, xii, 4, 29
adjunct, 16-17, 20-21
administrative progressivism, 7-9, 11, 14, 22-23, 25-26, 34, 48, 62, 125, 131, 139
Advanced Course of Composition and Rhetoric, 71
American College Literacy Crisis, 14, 16, 18, 21
assessments, 14-15, 48, 105, 115-117
associations: American Association of University Women, 97; North Central Association of Colleges and Secondary Schools, 37, 48; Modern Language Association, 37, 97; National Association of Academic Teachers of Public Speaking, 12
awards, 63, 97

Baker, George P., 20, 44-45, 81, 108-113, 122, 126, 143
Barnett, Barbara, 29, 31, 117
belletrism, 11, 13, 71, 104-105
Berlin, James, xi-xii, 8, 12-13, 16, 38, 41, 50, 54, 57, 76, 124, 132, 136, 142
binaries, 28, 30-31, 83, 85

Brereton, John, xiii, 14, 16, 18-21, 49, 71, 77, 108
Briggs, LeBaron Russell, 18, 20, 112
Buck, Gertrude, x, xii, xvi, 34, 44, 54, 57-61, 74, 94, 119, 127, 133-134, 141
bureaucracy, xv

Carleton College, ix, 53
Carpenter, George, 45, 81, 108-113, 122, 126
ceremonies: nationalistic, 9
chair: department, xii, xiii, xiv, 17, 35, 50, 59, 61, 74, 91, 95, 111-112, 123, 125-127
Chicago Laboratory School, 29, 140
Clapp, Elsie Ripley, 29
classroom: feminist, xiii, 29, 32, 85, 117-118; structure, 67
Clifford, Geraldine, xii, 134, 143
colleges: liberal arts, xx, 105
Committee of Ten, 16-17, 19
communities: classroom, xv, 29, 46, 58; college, xiii, 62; writing, 27
composition: argumentative, 12, 110, 112-113; goal of, 27, 49; history of, xi, xxii, 127-128, 136; modern, 13, 34, 40, 46, 53, 117, 119-120; theory, 17, 28, 30, 33, 129

concepts: abstract, 13, 24, 46-47, 114; human, 5
conferences: Conference on Uniform Entrance Requirements, 37; Intercollege Conference on English Composition, 58, 74, 87, 89, 94, 97, 139
connected experience, 5, 23-24, 27, 29, 31, 33, 114
Conrad, Lawrence, 53
consciousness: national, 132; social, 124
contemplation: strategic, xxi, 67, 97, 112
continuum, 31; experiential, xiv, 23; intellectual, xviii
course catalog, 11-12, 41, 57, 69, 71-72, 102, 104, 113, 143
courses: elected, 75, 122; offered, 13, 50, 62, 74-76, 96, 102, 104, 108, 113, 126; required, 68, 75, 91, 103
critical imagining: xxiii, 34-36, 51, 64-67, 69, 97, 108, 112, 128, 137
culture: American, 4, 8, 125; liberatory, 117
current-traditional rhetoric, xvii, 7, 10-11, 13, 15, 22, 26, 28, 58, 66, 70, 72-73, 76, 88, 92, 108, 111, 126, 136, 139-140, 143

daybooks, 37, 44, 135
debate, xx, 12, 57, 70, 74, 76, 91, 103-104, 110, 113, 142-143; defined as, 110
debate clubs, 110
democracy, 6-7, 74, 82, 101
Denney, Joseph Villiers, 43, 45-46, 81, 140
Dewey, John, xiii, xv-xvi, 3, 5-7, 23-36, 38, 40, 43, 47-50, 56-60, 62, 73-74, 82, 92-93, 107, 114, 120, 128-129, 134-135, 139, 140-141
departmentalization, 12, 25, 65, 74, 76, 89, 96, 131
Dial, The, 18, 96, 107-108
dichotomy, 40, 125
discourse: academic, 30; analysis of, 10; civic, xix; public, xix, 74, 124; rhetorical, 54; sociohistorical, xviii, 129
documents: archival, xvi-xvii, xix-xxi, 61, 65, 95-97
drills: grammar, 13, 19, 35, 78; memorization, 16, 42, 49, 51; skill-drill, 27-28, 85, 117, 121
dualism: critiques, 30
Durant, Henry Fowle, 98-101, 103, 108

economic system, 26, 132-133
Effinger, Dean 63, 135
elements of: speech, 12
Eliot, Charles William, 17
elocution, 12, 57, 69, 103, 143
English A, 14-16, 20
English in American Universities, 18, 41, 96
English Language, the, 67, 76, 91, 96, 104, 113, 141
entrance exams, 14, 16-17, 19, 47-48, 58
environment, classroom, 25, 29, 42, 85
essays, 15, 17, 44-46, 71, 104
exposition, 10, 50, 104-105, 113, 126
expressivist pedagogy, 30, 77, 142

Faigley, Lester, 40
feminism, xviii, 28-32, 56, 131, 141

feminist, xvi-xviii, xxi, 28-30, 32-33, 55-56, 64, 85, 108, 117, 128, 130, 137, 141
foremother, 137
forms of: instruction, 13; writing, 10, 13, 67, 71, 132
frameworks: sociohistorical, xxi; theoretical, 129
Freeman, Alice, 100-102
Freshmen-year students, xx, 14, 20, 27, 43, 51, 92, 102-104, 107, 109, 113, 121-123, 126, 143

Geertsema, Margaretha, 29, 31, 117
General Survey course, 113
Genung, John Franklin, 68, 104-106, 121
German System, 102
Gintis, Herbert, 4-6, 8, 132
Giroux, Henry, 34
Godkin, E.L., 16, 18
Gold, David, xi, xix-xxi, xxii, 5, 128
Goodman, Russell, 23, 139
Goucher College, 75
grading, xx, 10, 14, 21, 34, 44, 58, 86, 109, 121
graduate education: programs, 36, 41, 50-51, 53-63, 97, 133-134, 141; seminars, 41-43
grammar: instruction, 11-12, 15-16, 35, 40, 56, 68-69, 78, 81, 111, 114, 121, 142; structure of, 28; writing process, 21-22, 28, 45-47
Grant, Zilpah, 67
Great Depression, 90, 130
Greenough, John, 18
Griffin, Gail B., xxii, 33, 137
group work, xx

habits: as writer, 39-40

Haight, Elizabeth Hazelton, 34, 58
Ham, Roswell, 90-91, 130, 143
Hart, Sophie Chantal, xiii-xvii, xix, xxii-xxiii, 3, 20, 34, 59, 94-95, 97-98, 102, 104, 107, 109, 111-127, 129-130, 133-137, 143
Harvard Overseers, 16
Harvard Reports, 16, 19, 49, 88, 140
Harvard University, xiii, xx, 13-21, 34, 44, 47, 49, 65, 69-73, 77, 88, 102, 106, 108-111, 124, 140-142
hegemonic models, 22, 66
Henry Street Settlement, 4
Herbart, Johann Friedrich, 4-5
Hill, Adams Sherman, 14, 18, 20, 68, 105-106, 112
Hincks, Sara, 58, 60-61
historiography, xviii
hospital squad, 11
Hull House, 4, 29
humanism, 10, 51, 70, 72, 75-76

illiteracy, 7, 17-18, 88
immigrants, 4, 8, 11
institutions: coeducational, xii, 70, 103, 134
intelligence testing, 25
internationalism, 125
Ipswich Seminary, 67-69

Johnson, Nan, ix, xi, 69, 105-106
Johnson, Ruth, 81-82
journal: dialectical, 21; field, 18-19; scholarly, xvi, 97, 112; student, 65, 89
journalism, 37, 50, 76, 104, 142
Jugend, 52
Junior-year students, 14, 68-69, 103-104, 107, 110

Kerlinger, Fred, 9

Kirsch, Gesa, xviii, xxi, 3, 35, 54-55, 64, 67, 95, 97, 128
Kitzhaber, Alfred, xi, xiii, 11, 13, 17-18, 20, 38, 45, 62, 105, 111

laboratory model: of teaching, 107
Latin, 67, 73-74
Leonard, Sterling Andrus, 54
lessons: developmental, 106; grammar, 13
liberatory learning process, 80-81, 117, 141
linguistics, 37-38, 51, 53-54, 96
literacy crisis, 14, 16, 18, 21
literate: class structure, 4, 7, 67
Lockwood, Helen Drusilla, 61, 130
Lockwood, Laura, 129
Lyon, Mary, xix, 66-71, 76, 78, 89, 91-93, 98-99

Mann, Horace, 23
mastery, 31, 82, 108
memorials, xvi, 37, 43, 46, 51, 55, 58, 65-66, 79-80, 84, 98
Michigan, University of, xiii, 34-37, 39, 41, 43, 46-55, 57-63, 65-66, 73-74, 76, 95, 99-100, 107, 112, 116, 122, 126, 133, 135, 141-142
modes: distinction of, 51, 71, 105
Morrill Land Grant Act of 1862, 7
mother-teacher, 33, 83
Mount Holyoke College, ix, xii, xvii, xix-xx, xxii, 54, 57-59, 61, 63-77, 79, 81, 83, 85, 87-95, 98-99, 104, 106, 109-110, 124, 126-127, 133, 135, 141-143

narration, 10, 50, 71, 104-105
National Council of Teachers of English, 12, 37, 54

NCTE (National Council of Teachers of English), 16, 37, 54, 74
New Jersey State Teachers College at Montclair, 53
norms: behavioral, 7; collegiate, 11; cultural, 8
nurturers: women as, 32

objective observation, 13; powers of, 5, 46
oratory, 57, 104, 110
Oratory: Professor of Rhetoric and, 20
organizations: reform, 56
Origins of Composition Studies in American Colleges, xiii, 19
orthography, 12
Oswego Movement, 5

Palmer, Alice Freeman, 100-101
Palmieri, Patricia, 96, 99-103, 106, 108, 124-125, 129-130
participatory learning, 28-30, 32, 82, 85, 117
patterns: historical, 129; of action, 65
Payne, William Morton, 18, 41, 96
pedagogy: courses, 7, 81-82, 106; Deweyian, xiii, xiv, 25, 28, 30, 32-33, 38, 41, 45, 57, 83, 95, 101, 106, 119; feminist, 29-30, 32, 85, 117; progressive, xiii-xiv, 28, 30, 35, 42-44, 53, 57, 61, 79-80, 85, 93, 101, 117, 127, 129, 134, 142
Pestalozzi, Johann Heinrich, 4-5, 23, 67-68
philosophy, xviii, 23, 25-28, 46, 59, 73, 81, 96, 111, 114-115
Philosophy of Style, The, 105
plagiarism, 87
political activist, 99, 102

politics, xix, 4-5, 8
poststructural theory, 30
power of writing, xix, 9, 30-31, 35, 43, 47, 68, 77-78, 81-85, 114, 125, 132
Practical Rhetoric, 105
practices: educational, xiv, xvii-xviii, xxi, 3, 12-13, 22, 34, 39-40, 48, 58, 78, 92, 95, 106, 109, 124, 128-129, 139-140
pragmatism, xviii, 23-24, 28-30, 36, 139
Pragmatism and Feminism, 28
pre-writing, 46, 82
principles: of education and rhetoric, 6, 12, 42, 47-48, 50-51, 105, 116
Principles of Argumentation, 110, 143
Principles of Rhetoric, 105-106, 112
Principles of Success, 42
Progressive Era, xi-xvii, xix, xxii, 3-4, 10, 26, 29, 31-32, 34, 37, 54, 57-58, 64-65, 82, 97, 124, 126, 128-129, 131-132, 134, 136, 139, 141
Progressive Movement, xv, xviii, 3, 7, 56, 92, 121, 131-133, 140
progressivism, xiv-xvi, xviii-xix, 3-8, 11, 56, 75, 77, 130, 132, 134, 137; administrative, 7, 9, 11, 13-14, 22-23, 25-26, 34, 48-49, 62, 125, 131, 139; Deweyian, 22-23, 28, 30-32, 34-35, 38, 55-56, 75, 92-93, 120, 126, 132, 139-140; educational, 4
prose, 72, 84, 140
Prose Style, 76, 104
protégé chains, 55, 61, 133-134
psychology, 5-6, 38, 51, 54
punctuation: rules of, 35, 40, 46, 105, 111

Quackenbos, George Payne, 71
Quincy, Josiah, 16
Quinn, Patrick, 126

radicalism, 102
Randolph-Macon College, 75
Rankin, Thomas, 53
reform: educational, 5, 8, 38, 57; labor, 56-57, 134; moral, 100; social, xv, 4-5, 56-57, 100, 102-103, 124-125, 130, 134
relationship: student-teacher, 57-58, 83-84, 101, 125, 137
Report of the Commissioner of Education, 90
research institutions, 65
review: peer, xx
Rhetoric and Reality, xi-xii, 8, 38, 50, 54, 57, 76, 124, 132
Rice, Joseph Mayer, 23, 45
Riis, Jacob, *How the Other Half Lives*, 4
roles, xxii, 5-8, 11, 15, 29, 32-33, 84, 93, 98, 101, 119, 125, 127, 129-131, 134-135, 143
Royster, Jacqueline Jones, xviii, xxi, 3, 35, 54-55, 64, 67, 95, 97, 128
rubrics, 10, 21
rules of writing, 28, 116
Russell, David, xi, xv, 10-11, 14-16, 111, 131-132, 139

school reform, 8
school system, 6, 28, 133
Schooling in Capitalist America, 5, 132
schools-elementary and secondary, 5-6, 8, 11-12, 16-17, 28, 49, 121, 133, 140
science, 8, 10, 23-24, 111
Scott, Fred Newton, xii-xiii, xv-xvi, 17-19, 21, 28, 30, 34-56, 58-63, 74, 76, 78-79, 81-82, 92, 95, 97,

107, 111, 114-116, 119-120, 124, 129, 133-136, 140-142
sections: lecture/discussion, 109, 117
Seigfried, Charlene Haddock, 27-28, 32-33
Seminary in Advanced Composition, 41
senior-level students, 68-69, 81, 88, 103, 110,
settlements, 4, 56, 97, 103
Seven Sisters Colleges, xi, xiv, xix, 55-57, 62, 65, 98, 110, 141
Shafer, Helen, 102
shortage: of instructors, 122
Smith College, 57-58, 74, 87, 91, 95, 98, 100, 133, 141
Snell, Ada, 54, 61, 66-76
social: circulation, xxi, 46, 53-55, 94-95; consciousness, 124; construction, 28, 85; reform, xv, 4-5, 57, 102-103, 124-125, 134
socialist, xix
socialization, 7-8, 11-12, 22, 29
society: American, xv, 4, 8; democratic, 38; industrial, 7
sociocultural, xxi
sociology, xvi, 6
Socratic, 50, 58-59, 79
sophomore-year students, 14, 103-104, 107, 113
speech, 12, 48, 75
standardization, 7-12, 22, 25-27, 38, 47-49, 83, 131, 140
Starr, Ellen Gates, 4
Stevens, Clara, ix, xii -xvii, xix, xxii-xxiii, 3, 31, 34, 59, 61, 64-67, 73-86, 88-95, 97, 112, 114, 117, 125-127, 130, 133-137, 142
Stewart, Donald, 36, 42-43, 45, 47, 52, 141
Stewart, Donald and Patricia, 36, 38-40, 49-50, 54, 62-63, 111

strategies: learning, 119; teaching, 102
student knowledge, 11, 22
student-centered, 70, 76, 93, 142
student-teacher, 21, 58, 84
syllabi, 38, 65, 70

teacher-listener, 117
teaching loads, 20, 91, 123
teaching methods, 9, 19, 21-22, 37, 42, 50, 72, 85, 90, 108, 117
textual, 40
themes, xx, 12, 14-17, 19, 21, 34, 43-44, 52, 57, 71, 107-109, 113-114, 118-121
traditionalist, xvi, 9
trustees, 98-99, 102, 143
Tyler, Caroline Goodrich, 70

undergraduate, xii, 49-50, 57, 76, 84, 114
Vassar College, 54, 57-61, 74, 87, 94, 98-100, 110, 123, 127, 130, 133, 135, 141
Victorianism, 5

Walker, Danna, 29, 31, 117
Wellesley College, xiii, xvi-xvii, xix-xxi, 20, 57-59, 63, 74, 87, 94-113, 115-117, 121-127, 129-130, 133, 141
Wendell, Barrett, 19-20
West Hall, 51-52
Wheaton College, 75
Wiley College, xix-xx
workshop, writing, 26, 41-44, 53, 107, 199-121, 143
World War-I and II, 90, 130, 132, 143
Wylie, Laura Johnson, 60-61, 123, 127

Yost, Mary, 59-61

About the Author

Lisa Mastrangelo is a Professor of English and Women's Studies at the College of St. Elizabeth, in Morristown, New Jersey, where she teaches courses in composition, creative non-fiction, and research writing. Her work on Progressive Era instruction and archival research has been published in *Rhetoric Review, Rhetoric and Public Affairs*, and *College English* and in several edited collections. With Barbara L'Eplattenier, she co-edited *Historical Studies of Writing Program Administration: Individuals, Communities, and the Formation of a Discipline* (Parlor Press, 2004), which received the Best Book Award from the Council of Writing Program Administrators.

www.ingramcontent.com/pod-product-compliance
Lightning Source LLC
Chambersburg PA
CBHW032026230426
43671CB00005B/212